A Successful Formula

Reginald Murray

Copyright © Reginald Murray.

All rights reserved. No part of this book may be reproduced in any form or by any electronic or mechanical means, including information storage and retrieval systems, without permission in writing from the publisher, except by reviewers, who may quote brief passages in a review.

ISBN: 978-1-64826-526-6   (Paperback Edition)
ISBN: 978-1-64826-527-3   (Hardcover Edition)
ISBN: 978-1-64826-525-9   (E-book Edition)

Some characters and events in this book are fictitious. Any similarity to real persons, living or dead, is coincidental and not intended by the author.

Book Ordering Information

Phone Number: 347-901-4929 or 347-901-4920
Email: info@globalsummithouse.com
Global Summit House
www.globalsummithouse.com

Printed in the United States of America

CONTENTS

Introduction vii

Chapter 1:   Give It Your All 1
Chapter 2:   From Simple Minds Come Enormous Ideas 15
Chapter 3:   To Forgive and Forget? Why Not Both? 32
Chapter 4:   Got Problems? Then Welcome Them 39
Chapter 5:   Be Nice, Not nasty 54
Chapter 6:   A Consistent Concept 57
Chapter 7:   Overcoming Verbal Abuse 65
Chapter 8:   Mind Your Own Business 81
Chapter 9:   Dealing with Rejection 83
Chapter 10: Violence No More 90
Chapter 11: A Good Thing from a Bad Situation 105
Chapter 12: Mistreatment 115
Chapter 13: The Boy Who Could 125
Chapter 14: An Attitude with Latitude 131
Chapter 15: Push 141

Conclusion 147
Bibliographies 149

INTRODUCTION

Life as we know it can be an unpredictable phenomenon, as unexpected as the weather in March. Sometimes, we go through different phases for different reasons. Life will allow us to experience its ups and downs, its highs and lows, its unexpected turn of events which is as diversified as the clothes in a clothing store, as well as its stableness. Everything we encounter is for a specific reason. Our life expectancy enables us to stand tall against any adversity or pitfall that may come our way. It's just another way of preparing us to deal with its tough, cruel, harsh, brutal side mentally and emotionally. It can bring to the table some tough, imposing questions that are either answerable or unanswerable. It leaves a path for others to follow, instead of designing our own courses, and to face the many challenges that lie ahead. In short, our lives can be preemptive.

For instance, scientists and physicists can determine why an apple does fall far from an apple tree. Could it be that the weight of the apple allows it not to fall far from the tree? Or is it just one of the laws of averages? They have been pondering this difficult question for many years. They have unraveled the truth. Some of these truths are you can't change gravity, it falls in a vertical fashion, and it's too heavy to land on a flat surface. There are still many other possibilities to explore that only time can eventually reveal. These are just a few examples to back this theory. Another example is why a squirrel can run across a live wire and not get burned. If you or I were to touch it, that's another story. Or why is it that certain marine animals can live on both land and in the water while man has to survive on land? What is the purpose of a weed plant that grows haywire around your house, backyard, or between sidewalk crevices, giving off an ugly appearance? Why do poisonous plants like poison ivy and poison oak have no beneficial effect to man? One small touch of these toxic plants and we will feel its repercussions for quite some time. Moreover, a deer can carry that dreaded Lyme tick on its skin, but it comes away harmless. But if that same tiny arachnid touches our skin, we shall feel its repercussions, possibly to the point of death. If pushed from a certain height off of an object, why does an ordinary house cat always land in the same position? Again, if you or I were pushed, that's a whole new ball game. Lastly, why haven't chemists, scientists, and doctors found a cure for the common cold, flu, or headache in this sophisticated day and age of modern medicine? It can be treated, but it's a recurring problem. These are just a few difficult questions to ponder.

At the other end of the spectrum, our longevity has sometimes rendered us with some answers to life's most difficult questions. A prime example is how a snake's venom can be a lifesaver as well as a life taker. A known chemist discovered that venom could be converted to anti-venom, an excellent antidote for relieving pain. The lion is a savage carnivore and an extremely smart animal when selecting his meal for his cubs. He wants only the very best meat when he is out for the hunt. In addition to the killings, he will kill other big game cats, if they cross his path. He won't consume them for his meal because he knows he is in stiff competition for his food supply. Lastly, some of these predatory cats are highly intelligent to not let man tame them for their own good. They will remain in their natural state of environment. And we fellow humans have a tendency to act in the same fashion as some of these four-legged creatures do but to a lesser degree. Another way of paraphrasing it is our behavioral patterns are quite similar to these aggressive, savage beasts. For example, some animals will flee from their adversaries, if threatened or if their territorial rights are invaded. However, others will defend their cause to the bitter end. Don't we humans act out our irresponsible, irrational behaviors from time to time? I would be remiss if I didn't tell you that most of us could be more tactful, diplomatic, and could use some protocol when proving a valid point to others to further justify their cause. Again, let us take the case of the lion. Little does anyone know that if provoked by his own kind, he will also destroy them just to protect him, his cubs, and mates for their survival? In the same light, how many times have we become annoyed, disgusted, and impatient with each other's ways just to win one over to our way of thinking?

The correlation I'm trying to make between man and animal can prove quite fruitful and intriguing in establishing a healthy, harmonious, and happy relationship among us. To an extent, man does have a tendency to behave in the exact same fashion as other living creatures do. The Bible strongly admonishes to us that man's emotions vacillate like a swinging pendulum. He may welcome you with open arms one day. The next time around, he may not let you stand within a five-mile radius of his presence. Again, some questions to ponder are, "What causes man to act the way he does?" and "Is his environment a central factor in the making of his persona?" and "Why does he react in an irrational way to prove a valid point?"

As stated in the preceding paragraph, the main point I'm trying to convey is we will all have a clear picture as to why our terms of existence operates the way it does. In this fast-paced, changing and growing society we reside in, nearly everyone's goals, motives, and objectives are basically the same and different. We all travel different paths. By the same token, we all travel the same road to reach our ultimate destinations in life. We experience the joys and ecstasies, the highs and lows, and the rewards and repercussions that life offers. We are living witnesses to the demands and perils of life in which we experience. My point is we have all concocted different formulas and notions as a motivational tool for defining what our success is. It's a formula that you've written to experience the changing times of life. It has plenty of value and merit associated with it. It's written in the chronicles of life. It's etched in stone. It's called a winning formula. Another sophisticated way of calling it is a successful formula. That's why I've decided to title this book *A Successful Formula*. This is a new edition on making progress in your journeys and in establishing a salubrious affinity with one another.

Some of the chapters include dealing with problems, how forgiving is a moot point, how enormous ideas have evolved from basic minds, overcoming verbal abuse, and not using violence as a mechanism to prove your point. Moreover, we take an in-depth look on dealing with rejection, mistreatment, and whether your situation is favorable or unfavorable. Finally, I conclude with chapters focusing on an attitude adjustment and investing in the power of that all-mighty tool, prayer. There are many more chapters to cover. I've just mentioned a few, which might strike your interest.

I've given you a synopsis of how certain animals, plants, arachnids, and, of course, the strong, indomitable spirit of man collaborating in this wide-open world. I enjoy writing to help others by expressing my perspectives and ideas verbally on paper. I enjoy writing to relieve the drudgery of inactivity. It is the asset I use as a fundamental building block to instruct others to live a constructive, optimistic, and meaningful life in sustaining their goal. There are many who are at the bottom of the barrel. They don't need to feel our venom to motivate them at a second chance. That kind of medicine won't work. What will work are patience, prayer, and understanding to rejuvenate them. For instance, many have fallen prey to drugs that are infiltrating our society. Perhaps one has hit rock bottom while traveling this path. It made a drastic change in his life but in an unenviable way.

There have been other world-renowned authors, who were influential in motivating me to write this book. Some of them were Norman Vincent Peale, Dale Carnegie, and Doctor Leon

Howard Sullivan. Their messages were awe-inspiring, truthful, and strong. That made an instant impact on me and inspired me to help cure the diseases in this evil society. But the real impetus is to enable every reader with a broader and detailed perspective, which will underscore and have a valuable, positive, and lasting impression on him and his surroundings. There are a few more notable chapters to study, examine, explore, and take into account for your benefit. Everything we touch base upon should have a lot of significance in obtaining your sought-after goals. Enjoy!

ONE

GIVE IT YOUR ALL

To receive a certified public accounting license, one has to prepare rigorously for the twenty-hour examination. It can be mind-boggling, stressful, brain teasing, and, at times, both physically and mentally exhausting. The mental anguish begins with the steady grinding of studying long, endless, brutal hours, almost from sunset to sunrise. The midnight lamp burns incessantly. You have just received your four-year degree in accounting at some accredited university. The first half of the battle has been won. But the second half hasn't been decided. Now the real test begins. One has to really put his nose to the grindstone because, presumably, this will be his calling for the entirety of his life. One must know their material from all angles, if they are expected to elevate themselves in this profession. Every detail, big or minute, must be taken well into account. One has to step up to the plate and deliver. His hopes may soar to unknown heights. He goes in the room with all the cockiness, confidence, and swagger he could muster, thinking that he will pass the exam with flying colors. But then the letdown begins. After completing the gruesome test, he gets his results back. It's not exactly what he had in mind. Or another way of saying it is that he didn't quite measure up to the test's standard. Whatever the reason, it's back to square one. Everything you've prepared for has gone down the drain in one big swoop. You're left all alone, feeling hurt, somewhat bitter, confused, and frustrated. Perhaps, you feel the effort leading up to that particular day was not justified.

A prominent law-school student has earned their law degree and is ready to take that initial step in the real world and put their knowledge to use. Before doing so, he or she prepares for the five month drudgery that is the bar exam. Again, this test can be self-agonizing, tedious, and mentally draining. It's almost a half a year in advance. One has to give up a lot of his free time and activities that would, otherwise, be spent for his pleasure. You're left all alone in some isolated room. The months spent may be compared to a long time spent in some drug rehabilitation center. All of the hard studying and mental preparation boils down to how well you do on examination day. Again, the midnight lamp is burning for a specified period of time. Again, you skip meals just to push yourself to the limit. Again, you completely shut yourself out from the outside world and not socializing with your family, friends, acquaintances, and associates. Again, you deprive yourself of any leisure activity that would be to your benefit. And again, you fall short of your expectations, despite giving it 110 percent effort. Your confidence level has slipped somewhat.

The main point of my argument is not that you've failed in your futile attempt at becoming successful in whatever endeavors you practice. The point I'm trying to clarify is you gave it your all, despite pushing yourself to the limits. It makes no difference what avenues or procedures you took to maximize your potentials, because along with that will come a slight setback in pursuing your dreams. Along with being successful means having to pay a heavy price of hard work to achieve greatness. Success won't be handed to you on a silver platter. It most certainly will not happen overnight. Again, frustration, dejection, and hopelessness may bother you. You have been eagerly anticipating this golden opportunity at this juncture of your life. But you found out that reaching your goals is an uphill climb.

Now is not the time to sit back, fret, and mull over what happened or what might have been if you had taken a different approach. There can be no failure without trying. Some will flourish on their first try. It may be that their mental capabilities are slightly superior to others. Or they've had some hands-on experience in another capacity. Better yet, they know how to prepare for such a momentous occasion, thus, enabling them to see positive, amazing results. Whatever the reason, don't let your temporary setbacks sway you from making it. Give it your very best, and by all accounts, hang in there and give it another shot. Perhaps your ship has yet to arrive, but do some soul searching and dig down deep for that in-depth faith.

I can think of two places in the world of entertainment where people come, hoping for instant fame and glory, hoping to be in the right place at the right time, hoping to get discovered by random chance—New York and Los Angeles. In New York, many young aspiring actors, comics, actresses, singers, musicians, and poets flock to the streets outside the world-famous Apollo Theater, eagerly waiting for an once-in-a-lifetime chance to showcase their talents to the world. Many endless nights of rehearsing for their respective roles are used up in some lonely, isolated, deserted room. Moreover, their subjective prayers are included, hoping to be answered in a single call. The Apollo Theater's motto is, "One mike, one stage, one chance." It is the roughest audience in the world. It has been said that if you can make it at the Apollo, then you can make it anywhere. Backstage, the judges tell the contestants to say their prayers and do their best to everybody who is anybody. One must have lofty ambitions in the entertainment field if one is to make it big. The Apollo's point is if you dream small, there's no point at dreaming at all. One has to dream big in order to make it big. Some will be given a second chance to take their talents to another level or be given another shot at redemption. For instance, a gifted performer, who receives a phone call to perform on stage, has four chances to showcase their talents before a national television audience and pass the test on amateur night. If he does well, then he has won the hearts and affections of the eyes of the nation. But if he does horribly then he has disgraced himself publicly in front of everyone. In one split second, all of his hopes, dreams, desires, and aspirations turn to gray slush. However, never give in to negativity or self-denial because things didn't work out the way you planned them. There will be many other chances and avenues to explore.

Los Angeles, likewise, is another city where thousands of young gifted actors and actresses relocate, hoping to be made into instant stars on the big movie screen. Repeatedly, many long nights of practicing are spent in some secluded room, trying to make a good first impression on movie producers, executives, and directors, impatiently hoping against the odds of landing a part in some up-and-coming movie. It has been said that Hollywood is, supposedly, a place where the bright lights, sandy beaches, and festivities all glitter like gold. For people who are hoping to reach their destination in this oftentimes crazy industry, the road to stardom is no easy road. It may be for some. But for others, it could be an abrupt end to a promising career. In short, one finds out that "all that glitters is not gold." In a twinkle of an eyelash, his imaginary world has turned backed into a real one. He's been dealt a reality check. Perhaps one finds that he may have to go back to washing dishes, waiting on people in a restaurant serving food, working in a department store, or work in some other capacity that is not his first love. They gave everything they had. Still, they fell short.

In the entertainment industry, all is not peaches and cream on first try. Certain roles may be required for certain performers. In short, one hopes that in rehearsing for certain roles, they'll win over the audience's approval, because being in show business depends highly on the rating game. The newspapers, news media, press, and the public arena shall decide whether their accomplishments are justifiable or not. These young entertainers will be judged solely by experts, critics, and of course, frenzied fans like us. That's tantamount to saying that you endorse your product and hope it will flourish, not falter. These participants went to the four corners of the earth just to see the end results. New York and Los Angeles are the show business capitals of the world. One has high ideals, high hopes, high standards, high dreams, and high aspirations. Still, one may or may not always make it in this land of milk and honey.

I did say at the onset of this chapter that there were some people who went to great lengths to obtain their full potential and didn't quite get there. In this current paragraph, I am highlighting two prominent individuals as prime examples-one motivated to run for city council in the wide-open field of politics and the other in the area of accounting. Both reached their aspirations but not on their first tries, but they persevered and gave everything in their power. Both are the touchstones of success. They are Michael Nutter and John Milligan. Both of their roots trace back to Philadelphia. Their stories are quite remarkable and riveting. But first, we begin with Michael's.

Michael Nutter is the current mayor of Philadelphia. But to reach the acme of his political career didn't happen overnight. He kept at it and believed in himself. Michael is a man with plenty of dreams, desires, and visions. He is highly motivated by doing good and trying to make a positive impact on people's lives for their betterment. His parents raised him to believe that a good education and hard work are the fundamental driving forces to make society a better place. In addition, they instilled in him a flaming spirit to be a component for other people. It's all about the efforts for him and for others. Michael first ran for the city-council seat back in the late eighties and didn't win. But this young lion simply refused to quit. He used his defeat as a stepping stone to success. The second time around, he easily won the seat as a city councilman. It took hard work and a concerted effort for him to reach his goals. "You need people who can make a positive contribution," says, Michael, "people who are extremely motivated with good intentions and a strong desire to succeed. Surround yourself with positive people." During his fourteen years in city government, Michael has had regular contacts with everyday people, who need to have their lives improved drastically. Furthermore, he has expressed his opinion about the creation of laws, deleting ones that may be obsolete, and establishing new ones and speaking about different things that the local government should or should not do. "Some days, the job can be rewarding and beneficial. Other days, it can be somewhat tedious and demanding," states Michael. "Despite the pros and cons of being an elected official, all of this comes with the territory." Inspired by another city councilman back in 1983, John Anderson, Michael attended regular city-council sessions and was strongly influenced under his tutelage to run for public office. He helped John with his reelection campaign. The rest is history. And now, the John Milligan story.

John Milligan is a highly regarded, successful, self-motivated, hard-driven businessman. He works in the Philadelphia area and hails from a family of eight children. Having finished no higher than tenth grade, he enrolled in the navy, in 1968. While stationed in the navy, John received his GED and married at the tender age of twenty, in San Diego, California. Likewise, he enrolled at a junior college, and from that juncture in his life, he realized he had the potential to become an accountant some day. After serving two more years in the armed forces, John relocated to Philadelphia to go to Temple University full-time. He graduated magna cum laude in 1975. Shortly thereafter, he went to work for an accounting firm, Cooper and Lybrand, the largest accounting firm in the Philadelphia region. But his biggest challenge was facing the fact that he was the only African American employed by that company during that time frame. Moreover, it was even more of a challenge to deal with the white corporate environment in mainstream America. John decided to take the demanding CPA exam. It's an exam that one has to pass all four parts of to earn a license. The first time around, he did not pass due to his lack of study. On the second go-round, he studied most of the exam, passing three out of four parts. Still, he was a bit short of his expectations. Zig Ziglar once said, "Failure is a detour, not a dead-end street." By failing the first two times, it became a wake-up call for him. The third time was a charm. He passed all four parts with flying colors, thus enabling him the right to earn his certificate. Having stayed with the company for nine years, John worked his way up to manager. He served there for three more years, until he decided it was time to move on to greener pastures. Since the firm didn't have any significance, African-American managers or partners, this motivated John to go directly into business for himself. He made a bold decision to leave in 1984, did some soul-searching on his own, and decided to work for a minority CPA firm. He worked there for one year, and during his tenure, he realized that to reach your maximum potential, one has to start at the bottom and work your way up. Having confidence in his ability to get things done, this trailblazer ventured into business for himself. In 1985, he started in the basement with a portable computer and a typewriter, answered his own phone calls, and did some binding on his own. He opened his first office in 1986 and then, hired his first employee in 1987. Near the end of that year, he had four people working for him. The practice continued to prosper into the largest minority- owned firm, which is located in Philadelphia and elsewhere. John Milligan is a classic example of giving a new meaning to what leadership, hard work, perseverance, and determination will do for you. He didn't throw in the towel because he didn't succeed on his first two attempts at mastering accounting. John has earned his high marks, high praise, high honors and has received numerous accolades in recognition of his outstanding work to help the black community get back on its feet. He is truly one of the greatest accountants this country has ever produced. Of course, he pushed himself to the limits to see his results.

I gave you two classic examples of two fine, prominent individuals, who, by all accounts, are reaping greatness. Their unique experiences were, as a rule, their learning tree. We can profit from the paths they chose which will enable us to grow in our field of interest. Their knowledge will be passed down from one generation to another generation as a means of getting things done. You may not necessarily travel the similar roads they have taken, but whatever avenues you've explore, the final analysis is what matters.

The game of basketball, in and of itself, has made a fascinating turn in the wide, growing world of sports. It is in the market to compete with the other three major sports, over which one is the king of kings. It is a fast-paced game comprised of many golden chances of winning. And so it is in these next two electrifying stories that I want to share with you, as my reader, about two small-town colleges in the Philadelphia suburbs, who didn't have the most talented players on this planet like most big-name colleges do but possessed an iron will, commitment, and flaming desire to go to any extreme to achieve greatness. They are Villanova and Saint Joseph's universities. They may be small in some capacity but they are large in spirit and in other areas, enough to compete with the larger-scale schools to win a national title on the collegiate level. We travel to two different time spans with two petite colleges, who nearly turned their dreams into a reality by giving it everything they got.

The date was March 17, 1995. It may be a bit premature, somewhat unfair, or a cliché to say that both colleges were overachievers. That's a moot point. At any rate, my central point is that these tiny schools could contend with the big dogs for a national championship. It didn't quite happen that way. Let me tell you the story through my experiences. The Villanova Wildcats almost came away with one of the most stunning victories in college basketball history. As things transpired, it wasn't meant to be. Their opponent, the Old Dominion Monarchs, gave the national television audience one of the most awesome college-hoop shows this country saw. It had all the makings of a professional basketball playoff game. On this particular night, the game was won in triple overtime by the Monarchs, 89 to 81. That's not the issue here. The main issue is that two small teams gave a stellar performance, just to advance to the next round. It was how the game was played that really mattered. The Wildcats gave every inch of their muscles and every last drop of sweat to seal a victory, but the stubborn Monarchs didn't surrender. Consequently, it paid off in big dividends for them. The Wildcats were heavily favored to win. But because their foe refused to throw in the towel, Villanova was sent packing for the summer. At the end of regulation and the first and second overtime, the Wildcats had the ball at midcourt with about fifteen seconds left. Each time, Old Dominion managed to tie the affair, until the third overtime. Up until then, it was a seesaw affair. But then, the low-seed Monarchs ran away with the victory, earning the right to advance to the next round. Afterward, one of Villanova's superlative players, Kerry Kittles, said, "It isn't too many times a year you're going to play fifty-five minutes. We knew we had the potential of going real far. It was abrupt. It was very disappointing." Even the coach, Steve Lappas, said afterward, "I hope this is the hardest thing I ever have to deal with. I hope this is the hardest thing any of us have to deal with." One team was fortunate. The other was less fortunate, despite giving a stellar show and all that they had within their abilities to come away with a victory. Villanova could not put the final nail in her opponent's coffin, and each time, the Monarchs came back from the dead. In the end, it cost the Wildcats a victory and perhaps, another title.

About thirteen miles south of Villanova is another small-town college, Saint Joseph's University. The school's nickname is called the Hawks. It was in late March of 2004 that the team almost beat the odds. It was a tiny team with a big heart and a big mission to accomplish. The team was under the tutelage of a fiery coach by the name of Phil Martelli. How this team nearly rose to the occasion in dramatic style is beyond anyone's guess. Nobody expected them to come ever so close to making it to the NCAA Final Four Tournament. Nobody! The Hawks had no losses during its regular season and one loss in the postseason tournament, as one of its key players, Jameer Nelson, took one desperate shot with one second left on the clock and did not make it, thus hindering the team from going one round away from the Final Four. Considered by many as an underdog, the feisty Hawks lost to the Oklahoma State Cowboys, 64 to 62, narrowly.

The Hawks went through the regular season, beating their opponents convincingly, like a runaway locomotive train. The fans, press, news media, and players were astonished at how good they were. You can call it a magical season, but whatever the reason, this team played its heart out to the last second, just to gain respect, admiration, and attention from the basketball world. The Hawks had good coaching, team chemistry, and a dogged determination to win the national championship. Every player did his role and was supportive of the team. There were no finger pointing and no dissension. During the game, it was mostly a seesaw contest. The game was up for grabs. But with just under thirty seconds left in the matchup, one of the Hawks' players, Pat Carroll, drained a three-pointer, sending the Saint Joseph's fans into a wild frenzy. The miracle Hawks were only twenty-nine seconds—twenty-nine seconds—away from advancing to college basketball's elite four. But then, they were brought back to earth. The Cowboys' John Lucas reciprocated a three-pointer of his own with 6.9 seconds left. There was faint life left in the Hawks' stellar season, but it all rested on the shoulders of their stellar senior, five-foot-eleven Jameer Nelson, the tiny point guard who won the school's affection. With all the coaches and fans watching around the nation, Jameer took a seventeen-foot desperate jump shot that brushed off the rim, leaving the Hawks and their imaginary dream season in disarray. Sitting silently, stunned, dazed, and somewhat mawkish, Jameer and his team's magic carpet ride came to a bittersweet ending. Afterward, Coach Phil Martelli told the press, "At every level, I included, it's painful. The last game of the year is painful. Because of the setting we're in and the year that we had, there's no less pain." Maybe the basketball gods weren't smiling on the surprising Hawks at that moment, but there's no need to hang their heads in guilt, in shame, or beat themselves up, speculating over what might have been or any other possibility they could have taken. But with renewed optimism, Phil Martelli, Jameer Nelson, and the rest of the squad can look back and be thankful to have had a golden chance of making it one step closer to the finals, along with giving it their all.

Steve Lappas, Phil Martelli, Kerry Kittles, and Jameer Nelson were products of Villanova and Saint Joseph's University-two learning institutions, approaching the game with two different philosophies, from two extraordinary coaches and players the game has produced, operating from two different time spans. Both schools didn't quite complete their missions, amid giving a fine show of college basketball. Both universities have nothing to be ashamed of. They do not need an intense investigation of themselves as to what went wrong and why it happened. Both schools should not take their losses in vain. Whether you're a fan or not of both schools is a non-issue. The crux of my argument is they gave all the gusto they had to accomplish their desires. These schools were not in the same boat as other big-name schools nor was their talent level slightly superior to others, but they tried their very best to give their beloved fans a much-needed championship crown. It was a Herculean effort in trying to sustain what they were there for. There are two wise, old proverbs which says, "Never measure a man by his size but by his heart" and "It's not the size of the bulldog in the fight but the size of the fight in the bulldog." Who would dispute these sayings or criticize the work ethics of these teams? I would tend to think that these theories sum up everything about these remarkable basketball programs.

Any type of business or practice you aspire to be in has its rewards as well as its repercussions. Today, we live in a fast-paced, changing sophisticated society where everything has its assets, liabilities, values, and merits. These ingredients are essential in order to achieve excellence as your worthwhile recognition. Again, let us take the case of sports and, in particular, baseball and basketball. Too many professional sports teams have, literally, gone down to the four corners of the earth while trying to harvest greatness. Some flourished but many floundered. Some good representations are the 1964 Philadelphia Phillies, the 1969 Chicago Cubs, the 1978 Boston Red Sox, and the 1987 Toronto Blue Jays. They have all experienced near misses in attempting to attain their sought-after goals. Not only did they falter, but also they left an ugly impact on their respective cities. It is easy to sit back, point fingers, censor, and to some degree, lampoon these franchises and come to an unfair conclusion. And it is equally difficult to actually put yourself in the other person's shoes and see things from his perspective. Any job you desire—whether you're in business for yourself or with another client, whether you're are an individual sports person or are on a team—will, by all means, be your open-book story. At any rate, it would be an oversight on my part if I didn't inform you about my high school basketball team, the Olney Trojans, who, like countless other sports franchises, did not necessarily reach their maximum potential.

Spring is the season when there is hope, optimism, renewed faith, and revival of the mind, body, and spirit infiltrating the air. It was spring 1971, my last year in high school. Our hopes were soaring as high as an eagle soars, filled with prominence, expectations, and eminence. All of us were eagerly anticipating graduation day in order to branch out in the real world and see what life had to offer. Our high school diplomas were our graduation gifts. And so was our beloved basketball team. Like a city celebrating its champion caliber team, our team was also heralded the same way. We were handpicked by most experts and critics to win the city title. We posted a phenomenal twelve and two record during the regular season, beating nearly every high school with relative ease. Likewise, our playoff foe, the West Philadelphia Speed boys, had an identical record. But on a balmy Saturday afternoon, our roof caved in. In an unexpected turn off events, we didn't win it. The score was deadlocked at halftime. There we sat in the stands, mulling if our time had arrived or not with uncertainty. We won the tip-off in the second half with one of our players making a basket. But the lead was temporary because our opponent dominated us in every phase and aspect of the game, outscoring and outshining us from one end of the court to the other. We became a practice session to them. We were beaten in similar fashion, sending us home for the summer. In a twinkle of an eyelash, all of our hopes, dreams, and desires were shattered like broken glass. Another way of saying it is our "blue snow turned to gray slush." Years from now, maybe we can sit back, speculate, analyze, criticize, take it to the sixth degree, ask a thousand questions, and ponder over what should have transpired. It didn't happen that way. The Olney Trojans certainly have no reason to go around, wallowing in their despair because they gave everything within their limits to bring home the bacon. They sent a stern message to the basketball world that they could compete with any team at any time. They played their hearts out to the bitter end. And I've learned that one can never get too much heaven in this earthly life.

 Give everything there is to give within your God-given abilities to make the impossible become possible. Never take your true talents for granted. Rather, take them to the next level. There may be some temporary setbacks, pitfalls, and a few obstacles to hurdle in sustaining your goals. Pick yourself up, dust off your failures, and give things another try. Whatever form of business you desire, there will be some struggles along the way. But it's your learning tree, your gateway to the future. Each of us is unique with our gifts in life, which will help make this world a better place to reside in.

We are all blessed with some type of gifts to make our place a much better society than it was perhaps two or three generations ago. Don't give in to self-doubt, negativity, gloominess, or any other liability that may hinder you from achieving greatness. Because you went to extremes on your first few tries and didn't succeed doesn't mean your world will come to a sudden stop. You will be given a sea of chances to redeem yourself to complete your mission. One goes through different stages of life to enable one to grow and master his profession. Learn from your failures, try exploring new avenues, and in the long run, you will truly see remarkable results. You will be amazed at what's in store for you all this time.

Rule 1: *Don't undervalue your talents. They're all you've got to give.*

TWO
FROM SIMPLE MINDS COME ENORMOUS IDEAS

The next time you see someone drum up an idea that you feel is absurd, think again. Some of these ideas that have grown into prominence were from the minds of basic individuals. Very basic! Before their dreams were turned into realities, people back then probably laughed at these unique individuals. They probably laughed themselves silly or were in a state of hysteria, all because they thought their dreams would not flourish, or they painted them to be strange, so strange that they perceived them to be from another planet. It's just that their mental capabilities were far superior to that of the average Joe in terms of our standard of living. They were blessed with an extraordinary gift to turn nothing into something. It's very easy to sit back and point your finger at someone and say to yourself, "I could have thought of that myself." And you know something? More than likely, you're right. You very well could have. But you didn't do it. And if you could have, then why didn't you do it? What's difficult is to actually invent something out of the clear, blue sky. Don't kid yourself into thinking that it's easy to invent a device to better serve humanity because it never is. For certain people, it is. But for the majority of us, it never is. Be thankful for that person who dreamed up an idea to make life a little more convenient.

Many nineteenth-and twentieth-century African-American inventors were robbed of their fabulous ideas and were thought to be somewhat delirious due to the mere fact that they were nonwhite. But over the course of time, many saw that these inventions were far more than ordinary products; they were an asset to this nation. They helped America become the great nation that it is today. No one can ever refute the notion that these apparatuses, which came from black people's minds, that the ideas were commonplace in life. On the contrary, these innovations, which were thought of out of the need for survival, when America was practicing the cruel, inhumane system of slavery, were advantageous in help shaping her to be the vanguard nations of inventions. Soon thereafter, whites discovered that these concepts were more than just a mere idea-they were devices they could use to their advantage, making them billion-dollar profits. Because slavery was prominent during that time frame, many blacks were given limited or no credit or recognition at all. This was due largely in part to the fact that slaves were considered three-fifths of a human being compared to other races.

When one invents something, they can only hope that their device will flourish, not falter. Another way of putting it is every gadget that was ever invented did not necessarily work to the inventors, and did not work in helping us progress in life. When one endorses his product to the market, he can only hope that the consumer will find it most beneficial in aiding them. Make sure you're giving your customer exactly what he wants. Know how to endorse your product to the public. Trying to convince your buyer to buy your device means to look at his needs from all angles. It's a wide, open spectrum when taking into account the consumer's demand. Take well into account what will sell your apparatus, rather than leaving it dormant. You don't have to be the most talented inventor on the planet. Just know how your strategy will work.

One of the most prolific inventors east of the Mississippi River goes by the name of Jeffrey Dobkin, a mentor and author of the inventor's most resourceful book on marketing—*How To Market*

A Successful Formula

American Product For Under $500. And here is what he has to say about inventors who made it and those who didn't:

> "About ninety-five of inventors never make a dime with their inventions. The reasons? Most inventions are not commercially feasible. They won't sell or won't sell at the asking price. Also, most inventors have no budget to move the invention forward. To move an invention off the starting block requires money, time, and energy, mixed in with a good bit of dedication and drive.
>
> Another hindrance to successfully bringing an invention to the market is the inventor's lack of business experience and skills. Having a great invention and trying to market it are two entirely separate things.
>
> An invention is a spark, a flash of lightning in an eureka moment. It is a good snapshot in time and then, it's over. Starting and running a small business based on the invention is an entirely different experience that is played out over several years. Understanding the marketing function, budgeting, hiring, and management and growth are completely separate from the invention process yet are the most necessary parts of any successful small business.
>
> In fact, marketing skills may be more important than a good invention. I've seen many great products fail because of poor marketing skills and poor business skills. And I've seen some terrible products marketed skillfully that produced quite a great income for the business owner.
>
> Here's another example. An American may be a great architect—great designs, innovative

concepts—and still fail miserably, if he has no marketing skills, because no one will call him for any jobs. Conversely, a mediocre architect can be very busy consistently if he markets his services with good sound skills.

The same goes for inventions. Even if your invention is great, it doesn't mean you will succeed as a successful product in a particular marketplace. I had a client that had an awesome product—I know it was great because he demonstrated it to me. It was amazing. But it didn't sell in stores. It became just another product in a bin, on a shelf, next to another product on a shelf, just to the left of it, and another product on the right. No one knew what it was, and without the explanation and the demonstration, it quietly "died on the shelf."

Study your buyer, do your homework, and make sure you know what your product has in store for the market in general. In so doing, your device will soar to unlimited heights, to unknown expectations, in this wide-open world. Remember, whenever you market your innovation, make sure that you're giving the consumer precisely what he wants. Know what will work and what may backfire. Look at it from all angles. Take into account what will sell your apparatus, rather than leaving it dormant. You don't have to be the most talented inventor. Just know how to market your idea.

Was New York City a Thief in the Night?

It to a large extent is second nature in life when one comes up with a dazzling idea to showcase to the public, you can be twelve dimes on a dollar that that thief will cash in on the opportunity to steal one's belief and take advantage of one's belief and take it to a whole, new level for his or her own satisfaction, and say it was theirs, not yours. Better yet, one may steal another's concept and use it as a basis for another idea. When someone else steals your dreams, you are given limited or no credit or recognition, and it can be, at times, somewhat difficult to take back what is rightfully yours. Case in point is the history of skyscrapers occupying, the skylines of most American cities. New York City is a fine metropolitan area that offers a vast number of interests to suit one's taste. It is, by far, the most multiethnic, multicultural, and multiracial city in the world. To this very day, other cities look up to the Big Apple as a role model and inspiration, hoping to elevate them to the same level in the next century and beyond. New York does reach out to the public to enable them to grow. But did she steal another one's idea? The reason I am stating this is because Chicago, not New York, was America's first city in the world to invent the skyscraper, in 1890. The point of my argument is New York foresaw a fabulous idea to capitalize on. She liked it, stole it, took it to the ninth degree, and was thought to be the first-ever city to invent this idea. This is definitely not a putdown or being disrespectful to her. But let's be objective, fair-minded, and give credit where credit is due. Did New York steal someone else's dream and say it was hers? By all accounts, she did, but in a positive sense. Humans do steal from others from time to time to progress as far as they can or to make a fast buck to be able to afford life's luxuries. You'll never know who is watching what you are doing. If you do think up a remarkable concept, you would be better off to keep your thoughts to yourself before someone else discovers what you're doing, take off with your idea, receive all of the acclaim, and walk away with the grand prize. Be leery as to who is watching.

Why Steal Another's Idea?

It is a well-known fact that when one comes up with a remarkable thought, another person will try to steal your thunder and say it was theirs, not yours. Someone else will try to take off with your idea just to make a profit and will just literally "take the money and run." Whether your gadget is tangible or not tangible, patented or not, is beyond the point. The point is most inventors lack the capacity to protect themselves from con artists, fraudulent people, or just people in general. People will try to defraud you of your belief and apparatus if they can get away with it. A prime example is the person who invented the abdominal crunch machine. He didn't have enough capital to patent his device. Thus, another person saw what he was doing, capitalized on his conception, and amassed 125 million dollars in revenue. Of course, the original inventor made a profit of the same amount, but he had a rough ride in trying to reclaim his brilliance. The outcome was both parties wanted the recognition, both sued each other, and both came to a complete standstill. Such is the nature of the beast. To this present day, the person who invented the machine is unknown.

The Television and Fashion Industry and a Football Player

Television plays a major role at the expense of another's amazing belief. Most television programs depend largely on ratings. And to get a television audience to watch your shows, program directors, producers, and executives must hire someone who can come up with sound programs to keep their viewers enlightened, encouraged, informed, and entertained. Naturally, if one network comes up with a sound show that is an overnight success, then the other networks will follow suit to remain competitive. Other shows will become a by-product of that distinct, individual production. Either the shows will remain in existence or be cancelled due to a television mastermind.

Please bear in mind that in order for a highly successful show to remain on the air, it is strictly an in-house decision and the sole choice of the television board of directors, producers, and executives. People from around the country may call in with an influx of ideas on how to improve the quality of the show. But not everyone's ideas can be taken into account. The reason why most ideas are not feasible is because the public's line of thinking on improving the show(s) is different. A majority of these ideas are good; however, everybody's belief is not always accepted. All of this comes with the territory.

The fashion industry is a pivotal area for where the latest ideas and trends are invented and emulated from the public arena as a follow-up from the original inventor. A great representation is Elias Howe, the inventor of the sewing machine. Writer Mary Bellis is due credit for this remarkable story. Howe lost his factory job in 1837, relocated to Boston, and found work in a machinist's shop. It was there that he began tinkering with the notion of inventing a sewing machine.

Eight years later, Howe demonstrated his machine to the public. At 250 stitches a minute, his locksmith mechanism outstitched five hand sewers with reputations for speed. Elias Howe patented his device on September 10, 1846, in New Hartford, Connecticut.

For the next nine years, he struggled, first, to enlist interest in his machine and then, to protect his patent from imitators. His lockstitch mechanism was, quickly, adapted by others, who were developing innovations of their own. During this period, Isaac Singer invented the up-and-down motion mechanism and Allen Wilson developed a rotary hook shuttle. Howe fought a legal battle with these inventors for the recognition of his rights as the inventor winning one of his suits in 1856. The three inventors pooled their patented rights as the Sewing Machine Combination under which patented, machines were marketed for many years.

The first mechanical machines were used in factory garment production lines. But it was not until 1889 that a sewing machine was designed and marketed for home use. By 1905, the electrically powered sewing machine was in full-scale range. For more information, log on to *Stitches-The History of the Sewing Machines*.

What does a football player have to do with drumming up a fantastic idea? Well, it has something to do with it, to a certain degree, Nonetheless, the game has its fair share of ideas and innovations to make it that much more entertaining. The dimension of the game has changed dramatically from the days of its inception. To elaborate on my point, a tiny football player, Fred Gehrke, an art major in college, played for the then Los Angeles Rams professional football team. In 1947, he made a pen-and-ink sketch of a ram's horn and showed the rendering to the team's head coach, Bob Snyder. Gehrke suggested that the design would make an eye-catching addition to the team's helmets. The coach was still unconvinced, so Gehrke painted the design on the leather head gear. The following year, the Rams were the first pro team with a helmet insignia. In the days that followed, the logos allowed receivers to be noticeable downfield, when they were covered in heavy traffic. The quarterbacks could see their receivers. In addition, it was the early days of the forward pass. Thus, the logos made it that much easier for halfbacks and wide receivers to be distinguishable. Shortly thereafter, every high school, college, and pro sport teams put their logos and mascots on their helmets.

I should have known better. Through my personal experiences, I've had two people steal my ideas but on a minor scale. I went shopping for a new pair of sneakers, when, much to my surprise, another shopper noticed the brand I picked out. I was receiving plenty of compliments. No one even noticed what style he bought. What do you think he did? He decided against his first choice and decided to purchase the brand I chose. On another occasion, I was at a gathering with some friends. We were standing around, mulling, doing nothing. Even though I had just completed dinner, I wanted something light to snack on. I remembered that I brought an apple from home to satisfy my hunger. As I bit into it, another person saw what I was chewing on. To my surprise, he rushed out of the building, ran down the street to the nearest grocery store, and bought one. Some ideas can be very tempting. But the crucial point I'm trying to make is when one sees another come up with a super idea, he most certainly will rob him of his thinking for his own satisfaction. Such is human instinct.

Out of adverse situations great ideas can happen. Such was the case with Watch Night, the night before New Year's Eve. How this tradition unfolded is rather amazing. During the Civil War era, America was a nation divided into two separate countries, the United and Confederate States of America, respectively. Abraham Lincoln was the president of the Union states. During that time frame, many slaves stood around and waited for Mr. Lincoln to issue the Emancipation Proclamation, which would end slavery forever, on December 31, 1862. I conjecture that Lincoln wanted to wait the following day, just to have a new beginning. At any rate, slaves were freed, whether they were residing in the United States or drafted from Africa. Moreover, Lincoln urged all free slaves to enlist in the army to help fight for their eventual freedom and other slaves held in bondage, just to put an end to the war. It was a political move on the part of the president, but it was a just cause. Other members of Congress questioned the president's motives, but in the final analysis, the means justified the end results. Thus, Watch Night was born and became a national phenomenon.

Another prime example is how Mother's Day got started. I got this story off the internet at Mother's Day@123Holiday.net. It is a very moving story. It began nearly 150 years ago, when an Appalachian homemaker by the name of Anna Jarvis organized a day to raise awareness for poor health conditions in her community, a cause she believed would best be advocated by mothers. She titled it "Mother Day's Work." In 1905, Anna Jarvis, the mother, died. Her daughter, also named Anna, started a campaign to memorialize the lifework of her mother. Word has it that when she was young, she remembered her mother giving a Sunday school lesson on which she said, "I hope and pray that someone, sometime, will memorialize Mother's Day. There are many days for men but none for mothers." Having taken her mother's death seriously and those words reverberating in her ears, young Anna spent the rest of her life trying to bring her mother's good wishes into actuality.

She began to lobby to prominent legislators, executives, and businessmen on both the state and national levels, such as John Wanamaker and Presidents Taft and Roosevelt. Being a fluent speaker herself, she passed up no opportunity to promote her project. On the third anniversary of her mother's death, Anna handed out her mother's favorite flower, the white carnation, at her church in West Virginia. In 1914, her hard work paid off when President Wilson signed a bill recognizing Mother's Day as a national holiday.

People observed Mother's Day by attending church, writing letters to their mothers, and, eventually, sending cards and other trinkets. With this idea in mind, Anna became livid. She felt that the day's sentiment was being sacrificed for greed and profit. She did not succeed in preventing such an outcome. On one occasion, she was arrested for disturbing the peace at a convention selling carnations for a war mother's group.

Anna Jarvis passed away in 1948, but before her death, she had her doubts about starting the Mother's Day tradition. Despite Miss Jarvis's misgiving, Mother's Day has flourished into a national obsession.

Imagine you had the power to create your own city. What characteristics would you use to establish it? Well, there are many deciding factors to take into account. Unfortunately, I can't list all of them, but I can certainly try to start with the most basic steps to create one. This fact that I am trying to highlight may seem a bit puzzling. The main point of my argument is you've thought up a magnificent idea for surviving. I have gathered a list from the most important to the least important. And here is my list:

1. **Water**—that includes rivers, banks, lakes, harbors, seas, and oceans. Since all of our natural resources depend largely on water, why not start near a large body. All of the city's activities flow freely in and out by means of some kind of waterway. We use it to our main advantage. Let it be known that three-quarters of the world is covered with water. Water should be prime essential on your wish list.

2. **Land**—maybe one quarter of the earth is covered with land, but what type of land you settle on and where is a major factor. I'm sure you would prefer one rich in minerals because you would want to see your city progress for many, many years. Also, the location is central in serving you in your comings and goings.

3. **House**—we need to have a place of shelter to protect us from the elements of the universe, from the change of seasons, a place to secure our own privacy and space, for pleasure, personal reasons, etc. And what better way to start with a house.

4. **Hospital**—this is a contributing factor as a primary building block for a city or whatever illnesses we encounter. A hospital is vital. Without it, we will, slowly but surely, wither away back into nothing. We need a daily routine to keep us alive, active, and healthy for as long as possible, as vital part of our lives to keep us in existence. It is an asset, aiding us whenever we become sick or injured.

5. **Church**—whatever your faith or denomination is, a church, synagogue, or any other house of worship is an excellent example of praising your Creator and giving thanks for your gains in observance of the seventh day of the week.

6. **School**—it has been said that knowledge is power, that education is the key to laying the foundation for a better society. And all forms of education begin with grammar schooling. And how you progress with your wisdom—from elementary, to high school, to colleges or universities, and beyond—will vastly determine what type of society you long for. Education is forever.

7. **Names**—to put the finishing touches on your new city, you need to come up with a good name to remember it by. We create them for our beloved siblings and friends, for our household pets, objects, or what have we need to identify. If you did idolize someone famous or important, you would do so based on their accolades and merits. Perhaps, one has done great deeds in their life to be remembered by. After they have passed on, you would remember them for what they stood for. There are many names with many meanings behind them, and thinking of a great one puts a premium on your project.

Hospitals are always looking for new and innovative ideas to keep people above the surface of the earth, not from becoming extinct. Hospitals are looking for ways to improve the quality of one's living condition in the wide-open field of medicine. Considerable progress is being made to cure and treat various diseases, as well as to prevent them. But still, hospitals have a long way to go to aid in one's sickness. And it all starts with one area of concern that affects all Americans from all walks of life. And that major issue I'm talking about is our national health-care system.

Our health-care system is failing. It began with the politicians in Washington DC. Presidents, past and present, have opposed one another's theories over this subject. President Clinton has tried to address the health-care system. President Bush didn't have it on priority in terms of his agenda. Senators Arlen Specter and Rick Santorum are apathetic about the health-care issue and the needs of people, particularly the poor. People cannot afford medicine or the health-care premium. Some have to take a pill every other day, and some have to decide if they are going to eat or get medicine. This is crucial for a nation rich in resources and gifted in terms of its inventions. Yet, we can see how millions and millions of dollars go overseas to aid other people. There is nothing wrong with that. But first, we should start at home. Let us think about the aftermath of Hurricane Katrina and the damaging effects she left on millions and the city of New Orleans. Should individuals have to sit and wait for bus companies to take them out of the disaster area? When we think about the major sports games played here, buses are in line until the last person leaves. Until something is done about our health-care system, many people will die. The number of medical malpractices is sky high. An ob-gyn (obstetrics and gynecology) physician has to pay two hundred thousand dollars a year, when he doesn't even make two hundred thousand dollars a year. If you don't make two hundred thousand a year, how can you pay for something that is more than what you make when you haven't even paid for your overhead in your office or your telephone bill at your home? A lot of ob-gyn physicians have gone to work for pharmaceutical companies; some doctors have retired earlier, some are forced to get jobs in other areas of the health-care profession, and when decisions are made in the health-care profession, seldom do they ask doctors about their input. They should be asking doctors for their input on how healthcare should be managed, especially when it comes to their patients.

Big business has taken over. A pharmaceutical company has given free medication to doctors or to an individual who cannot afford medicine or don't have money to buy their medication. Sometimes, people will have insurance like Peace to pay for their medication for six dollars per prescription. But sometimes, they make five dollars above the cutoff point. Then they have to spend over one hundred dollars a month just for medication, which is extremely high. If we don't do something for our health-care system, many people will die. In a rich nation such as ours, it is unbelievable that we have allowed the health-care system to deteriorate the way it has done over the past few years. Medical students are not encouraged to stay in the Philadelphia region. There are five medical schools in this area. Eighty-two percent of trained physicians leave and go elsewhere. There are doctors who might relocate and go to the Southern states, where malpractice is much cheaper. If someone has to get a loan for two hundred thousand dollars and you don't make two hundred thousand dollars, you would never catch up. You would go deeper and deeper in debt. It may not be encouraging for youths today to go into the field of medicine because of the complaints they hear. If members of their family are talking about it in terms of health care, doctors are making less than they ever have made. It is not what you make, but what you have left, after you pay your essential bills, which applies to every profession, whether you're an architect, engineer, teacher, automobile mechanic, salesman, etc. One can only hope that someday soon, there will be a big turnaround and change in our health-care program so people can be better served and can live longer and not die of neglect. And we should owe this to ourselves and to all citizens, regardless of race, color, creed, origin, or religion.

Before closing this segment of this book, I wanted to highlight someone of special interest to capture your attention. His unique inventions are the climax of this chapter, as I perceive. Once in a blue moon someone does come along with extraordinary talents that expand globally to take civilization well into the next century. You've heard of the likes of Imhopteh, who is dubbed the "father of medicine" or George Washington Carver, who discovered over three hundred different ways to make products from an ordinary peanut (medicine included), or the computer wizard, Bill Gates, who is labeled the "father of super computers." At any rate, his astounding gadgets have earned him the respectable right to be called the "father of the Internet."

A Successful Formula

Philip Emeagwali has earned his place in our hearts and in the annuals of time. Having risen from obscurity to prominence, some of his inventions are at the forefront of others. We are amazed at what a single individual can accomplish in so relatively short a time. He is well-ahead of his time, in his standard of living.

Philip rears from Nigeria, West Africa. Having mastered mathematics at an early age, young Philip had visions of becoming an Internet prophet some day. His father used to drill him to solve one hundred problems in an hour to help him pass school entrance exams. But his early schooling came to a sudden halt because his country was in a civil war of its own. He had to prematurely leave and enlist in his country's Biafran army for his survival. The war eventually ended, and he enlisted to attend school, again. But that was short-lived because he dropped out, due to lack of money. Eventually, he received his first diploma from the University of London in 1973.

As I've said earlier in this chapter, an enormous idea from a simple mind can grow into prominence; such was the case with Philip. He read a science fiction article on how to use sixty-four thousand mathematicians to forecast the weather for the whole earth. This article inspired him to work out a solution for using sixty-four thousand processors that were evenly distributed around the earth. He called it a Hyper Ball international network of computers. A more common name associated with this term is called the Internet.

As time went forward, in 1989, his formula to use over sixty-five thousand (65,536) binary computer processors, performing a phenomenal 3.1 billion calculations per second, gained him worldwide recognition. It was a task that was very rare for a scientist. Philip's remarkable discovery made front page headlines and cover stories everywhere. The feat broke previous computer records and proved that a small network of computers can outperform the large computers. Even academic journals, which formerly rejected his work, began lauding him on his idea. Even the big-name computer companies, like Apple Computer, were inspired to use his formula. Moreover, his formula can solve the world's most complex math problem.

Philip's idea opened the floodgates from nearly everybody in the four comers of this world, extolling him on his brilliant career. They range from computer scientists to journalists to celebrities. Even President Clinton praised him for his findings. The president gave a speech to the Nigerian National Assembly and here is what he had to say about this computer wizard before a televised audience, predated on August 26, 2000.

> "... one of the great minds of the information age is a Nigerian- American named Philip. He had to leave school because his parents couldn't pay the fees. He lived in a refugee camp, during your civil war. He won a scholarship to a university and went on to invent a formula that lets computers make 3.1 billion calculations per second. Some people call him the "Bill Gates of Africa."
>
> But I want to say to you is there is another Philip Emeagwal-or hundreds of them-or thousands of them-growing up in Nigeria today. I think about it when I am driving in from the airport and then driving around to my apartment, looking into the faces of other children. You never know what potential is in their minds and in their hearts, what imagination they have, what they have already thought of and dreamed of that may be lacking in them because they don't have the means to take it out ... "

Since then, Philip has received numerous awards, honors, and recognition for his worthwhile feats. Perhaps, this single idea will undoubtedly stand out in the minds of many computer experts in the Internet world, in the coming years. It will stick out like a sore thumb. In recent years, others calculations have surpassed his previous mark setback in 1989. But give Philip all the credit for his amazing idea. Most people think twenty or maybe thirty years down the road but not so for Emeagwali. He's already living in the next millennium. For further information, visit his website at Philip@Emeagwali.com.

Don't let your dreams die. Go after them in every possible way. Whether they are big or small, in the first degree or the tenth degree, pursue them to the best of your abilities and then turn them into reality. Most amazing ideas occur from the minds of ordinary people who are no more commonplace than you or me. Whenever God pours down his ideas from his windows of heaven, it is because he wants us to make his world the best that it can possibly be. Certain people are put in certain positions in life to make it more affordable. Take them to the next level in terms of living. You don't have to be someone of special interest or famous to make your dreams come true. Be the person you were meant to be. Carve out your own niche, and you will be content at what you have achieved. Dream big to make it big.

Rule 2: *Make your dreams as big as you can and pursue them.*

THREE

TO FORGIVE AND FORGET? WHY NOT BOTH?

Frederick Douglass forgave his slave master, the nefarious Thomas Auld, who, some 150-plus years ago, nearly succeeded in depriving him of his manhood as a slave. But before I proceed with this chapter, just look back at the list as to what Thomas did to him while he held him in bondage: he struck down his personality, he hired him out to a slave breaker to work like a beast, whipped him into submission, took his hard-earned earnings, sent him off to prison, offered him for sale, and so on. I could go on with this countless list as to other wicked things he did to him, but I won't. It is degrading and demoralizing how certain humans mistreat other humans in such a roundabout way just to defend their means.

In May of 1981, Pope John Paul II almost had his life taken away when a would-be assassin, Mehmet Ali Agca, tried to end it over something that he thought was politically incorrect. What do you think the Pope did? He went to the jailhouse and pardoned his adversary after a long slow recovery period of two years.

One person was almost beaten out of his senses. Another nearly had his life cut short, due to a single bullet. Most of us would have loved to see those who have severely tried to put a stumbling block in our paths to excellence be hung to die. An abolitionist and a Pope could have easily taken their traumatic experiences to their graves. They didn't. They chose to dismiss it like how water runs off a duck's skin. They overlooked what had transpired, in spite of their philosophical differences; they overlooked these idiosyncrasies as if they were moved by some divine intervention. Another way of saying this is they forgave and forgot. For most of us, it is a bitter pill to swallow. We mull over our sour experiences from here until eternity because someone did you an unjustifiable injustice. It is most unhealthy and unwise to become vindictive, to hold something against that individual, who may have tried to hamper you from progressing. It's very unhealthy because when you wake up in the morning, it can be a heavy burden on your mind to carry around with you throughout the day. You're in a heated debate with yourself as to whether you should overstep those that directly try to put a monkey wrench in your path or penalize them to the ninth degree, making them pay dearly for what was done to you. To hold malice against another person's wishes will only put you in a bad state of health and mind for the rest of your life.

It is unwise because you're climbing the ladder of success. Most of the time, what was done to you may have been done on a minor scale. People who practice these idiosyncrasies on another scale are, perhaps, green with envy. They will try from every possible angle to bring you down to their level. But you have to look past their weakness and keep going. What, if not revenge, is the ulterior motive for getting back at somebody? The great Indian philosopher Mahatma Gandhi once said, "An eye for an eye would make the whole world blind." Ignore them; they haven't got the slightest idea or clue as to what they're doing to hinder you from making it. Only a philistine would think as low as to think of such an out-of-the-way machination as to derail you. Forgive them anyhow, amid your hurts, your frustrations, and your pent-up anger.

Again, let us take the case of Frederick Douglass and his former slave owner. Frederick paid him a kindly visit in the latter years of his life. Thomas Auld was moribund, ready to step into the unknown eternal life. But before doing so, he uttered these kind words to Frederick. He told him, "Frederick, I always knew you were too smart to be a slave. Had I been in your footsteps, I would have done as you did." Those words echoed in Fred's mind, until he passed on to another life. Thomas may have injected his venom into his former slave. However, Douglass got over what was done to him, parting ways on a friendly basis, and never looked back. In other words, he forgave his nemesis.

To forgive and forget is likened to a balancing scale. Some can forgive, yet others cannot forget so easily. Few can do both. As with most humans, it's either one or the other, even though there is some ambiguity here. I, once, interviewed a pastor by the name of Steve Garstaad, and he shared some of his thoughts with me on forgiveness. He told me that the human spirit wants amnesty, not amnesia. The scripture teaches that God forgets our sins. He, then, explained that our behavioral patterns have consequences. That is why it is rather difficult to forget at times. The upshot of our behaviors can last forever. For instance, if I was a drunk driver and killed someone, then the family would grieve for that person forever, and it would be difficult to forget. Forgiving, on the other hand, is a different part of that human experience. Forgiveness is likened to a human journey. A pastor of a church committed adultery. It destroyed his family. The leaders of the church had to deal with that. He, eventually, left the church. The interim pastor challenged the session. He said, "Is there anyone here who doesn't believe that Jesus teaches us to forgive?" No one raised their hands. Everyone realized that it was the teachings of the scriptures. He furthered inquired whether some had forgiven or not. The response was fifty-fifty. The minister explained that forgiveness is like a train. Some are in the locomotive, some are in the club car in between, and others are in the caboose. Forgiveness is a journey. Most of us don't forgive instantly. It is a process and an important one. It's a burden we carry, until we are able to forgive and let go of that anger and resentment we carry around. And it takes emotional energy to fuel that. There are people who carry around past hurts or a shrine of pain. They become caught up in it. And it is not healthy for the human soul. Why some people can never forgive is something that no one can understand. They become a "prisoner of their own guilt and negativity."

Pastor Steve gave two examples of those who can let go and those who can't. A preacher by the name of Spencer Smith had a teenage daughter, Pam, who was struck down by a motorist while she was coming home from a park with some friends. The following Sunday, her family received word that she had died due to fatal injuries. Meanwhile, he was in the pulpit preaching the word of God. That afternoon, he went to the home of the man who had been driving the car, which struck the girl, and offered his forgiveness and consoled the man. This gave him a release, a release he never experienced before.

On another occasion, Chuck Colson told a story in his prison ministry. He and a judge Brewster were visiting a prison in Indiana. They were in the cell of a prisoner who committed murder and who was on death row. Chuck Colson was nervously looking at his watch because he had to leave and catch an airplane to fly to the Capitol and visit with the governor. He told that to the judge. The judge then turned to him and said, "I sentenced this man to death. But because he was a brother in Christ, I forgive him. And now, I pray with him." This was an awesome story.

And still yet, another wonderful example is that of baseball slugger, Barry Bonds, of the San Francisco Giants. Bonds once remarked that he can forgive but not forget because of the allegations stemming of him and his use of steroids to enhance his performance. Those accusations probably affected his reputation as a clean-cut ball player. Words can sometimes have a negative and devastating impact on a person, and it takes time to recover from the damaging effects, like a cut slowly healing from a festering wound. Our words are who we are and what we stand for. Perhaps, our criticisms are slightly off-base when we heap them on our fellow humans. We should practice more protocol in our daily contacts.

Can you forgive yourself? This may be a vague, but a just question. You would want others to forgive you, just like you forgave them, thanks to their circumstances. You've probably made some left turns in life, and you want a little redemption for yourself. For example, you may have abused your physical body somewhat with drugs, alcohol, craving for too much sweets, etc. Or you may have done someone a disservice on purpose, probably broke some laws where you had to be incarcerated for a specified period of time. In any case, can you forgive yourself? Of course you can. Don't doubt your unlimited potential to overcome your liabilities. All of us are born with some shortcomings in life. But that doesn't mean we should let them get the best of us. It is a personal challenge to see if you can pardon your wrongdoings, learn from them, and move on. It's all about making you a well-rounded person and uplifting your spirits. Also, it will enable you to help other persons become more knowledgeable and noble. One of life's main laws is to rectify our own infirmities and grow wise from it. You are being fair with yourself by getting another shot at improving your quality of life.

Is Revenge the Answer?

Again, this may be an honest and straightforward question, but it is a challenging question. Is getting even at someone always the right thing to do? The answer is no. Revenge should never be at the top of anyone's list love or hate list. In fact, it shouldn't be on anyone's list at all. Becoming vindictive is never the right thing to do. Many still believe in the old "eye for an eye and a tooth for a tooth" method. There are many people who have no respect for life or for anyone or regret what they have done to others. Moreover, they become fed up with themselves, almost to the point where they will, sometimes, use foolish tactics to bring others down to their level. Many spend sleepless nights thinking of some off-the-wall diabolical scheme for getting back at those who did them severe injustice. Those who hurt others were hurt so badly themselves that that's all they know. Never use revenge as your ulterior motive just to prove your point or try to win another to your way of thinking. If you do, you become cruel, childlike, indifferent, and insecure. Trying to harm another's reputation will only make matters worse. Getting even can only cause you to dig a deeper hole for yourself. In addition, it may cause others to disassociate themselves from you. A movie, *Fiddler on the Roof*, had a clever one-liner. It said, "If everyone practiced an eye for an eye and a tooth for a tooth, then no one would have any teeth left." There is no clear-cut, definitive answer as to why people still want to invest in the revenge motive. Anyhow, do away with your revenge tactics. It should never be on your priority list.

The *PBS* network once did a mini-series called *The West*. In it, the narrator, Peter Coyote, shared his thoughts on what the West was really like. Back in the old days, when America was expanding herself from the Atlantic to the Pacific Ocean, many migrated out to the wide-open West to seek out a better life, better fortune, and some adventure. The West was thought of as a high-drama, action-packed place. It was a place where cowboys and Indians would square off, where gunmen would kill off each other, with such malice and contempt over greed and wealth, bounty hunters posted rewards of people dead or alive and where stage coaches, covered wagons, and nasty saloon fights spilled over into the dusty, lumpy streets. Such were the characteristics of her persona. But Peter felt the real impetus of the Wild West was perceived to be a healing ground. It was a place where others could be given a second chance at life for all of their wrongdoings. Other parts of the country would have condemned these miscreants for what they had done, according to the laws of society, but not so for the unknown West. She was intent on giving the bad apples a second chance at redemption. Their slates were wiped clean and they had a new beginning at living. To put it mildly, the West forgave and forgot their intrinsically mortal sins.

Is there a place in your heart to forgive and forget? By all accurate accounts, there should be. There is no point in doing one and not the other. That's equivalent to dieting and not getting enough exercise or vice versa. If you exercise but don't diet, you would lose inches but not pounds. Likewise, if you diet but do not exercise enough, you would drop pounds considerably, but you would appear skinny and emaciated. One does compensate for the other. The same argument is central in pardoning another's flaw. In each of us, there is a subconscious force to free us from the shackles of vindictiveness. It is up to us as unique individuals to release these forces and uplift our minds and spirits. Overlook the harm inflicted upon you by another person and forgive them. The minute you forget them, they are out of your book of life forever. In the first place, they were probably clueless as to why they did what they did. Norman Vincent Peale once said, "A man is what he eats, a man is what he sleeps, a man is what he thinks, a man is what he is, and a man is, also, what he forgets." The last word, "forgets," is a strong one to retain. It means to let go and move on, despite what was done to you. Don't retain any negative thoughts toward your nemesis. Overcome them somehow and move on with your life. So do yourself a big favor and forgive all that may have spitefully done you wrong and learn to forgive yourself as well.

Rule 3: *Forgive someone totally and completely. Forgive someone and set yourself free.*

FOUR
GOT PROBLEMS? THEN WELCOME THEM

Let's assume that you live in a city named "X" comprising of a population of two million people. And for every person in that city, I assign a unique problem for each. Two million people mean two million problems to deal with. They can be minor or major, tangible or intangible, depending on your factor. Some you can handle right off the bat. Others may take awhile to resolve. Still, other problems may seem like an eternity to settle before you come to a justifiable conclusion. One thing is guaranteed: you will have problems to live with for the remainder of your life because the world is full of them. There's not one place in this world where no problem exists. True, you were put here for a specific purpose, but at the same rate, each of us has our own unique paradox to address to the best of our abilities. And that can range from repairing a tiny household appliance to repairing your car. It can range from sewing the buttons on your shirt to remodeling your kitchen, from nursing a small cut to preparing for major surgery, from making some adjustments to a small social club for our pleasure to making major ones to some national honorary chapter. However, because you have a specific conundrum doesn't necessarily mean you should go around mulling over it 24/7, or making it seem like you're working for the Pentagon. Stay with your circumstance, by all means.

What is a problem? A problem is a burden or trouble we all have deal with. There are no shortcuts or easy streets to take in solving one. But there are preventive measures to take in order to defeat it. It can take a great deal of time, concerted effort, and thought to come to a justifiable conclusion. It can range from on a local scale to a worldwide scale. Likewise, wherever you relocate on this earth, you would run into a similar or a different problem. And what do they mean? It means that each poser you handle is for a specific reason. There are different problems associated with different people. For example, you are given a unique one by your Creator because he knows your circumstances. One person may not be strong enough or possess an iron will to overcome his. Yet another individual may be better suited for conquering his with relative ease. At any rate, stay with yours and learn from it.

There are many balances in life to contend with, unfortunately. Out of the ones we know, the most common ones that stand out are our homes, schools, jobs, and churches. They will enable us to grow, learn, and better cope with the brutal side of life. First, let's begin at home.

1. **Homes.** This noun has many pitfalls, loopholes, and other adverse conditions it may throw at you. However, this can, sometimes, result in certain family members becoming envious of their siblings and their accomplishments. This can result in certain brothers and sisters becoming alienated from each other. They may not speak or pretend that neither exists. Sometimes, they can turn on each other. It may lead to all kinds of problems that need to be fixed. Moreover, certain children may turn to drugs, excessive amounts of alcohol, or have an uncontrollable craving for a lot of sweets. Another factor to consider is where your family is raised. Some neighborhoods are drug free, cleaner, safer, and more secure than others. For instance, if you are bringing up a young child, you

wouldn't want him or her to turn to drugs as a solution for their problems. Or you wouldn't want them to be involved in domestic violence or masochism to justify their cause. Both of these repercussions could result in a dead end. One would not desire this form of living. There are many liabilities at stake to take into account. In the long run, this may prove quite costly to one, in choosing the desired lifestyle for them. This is certainly a problem to consider. In this regard, your family is most important in helping you alleviate the pressures of the world.

2. **Schools.** As I've mentioned in the second chapter, schools or any learning institutions have its fair share of problems as well. Again, domestic violence has plagued many of our school systems across the nation. What's even more frightening is that pupils are at war with each other over things that are trite or egregiously silly. Classrooms were once thought to be a safe haven for learning. Not anymore. It's becoming like a war zone nowadays. Too many students are turning to weapons that can kill. For instance, if one student calls another one a dirty name or gives another one a foul look, they are ready to fight it out in fifteen brutal rounds. This has resulted in some matriculates committing senseless murders at a very early age, often in the form of school shootings. School bullying is a major concern. There was a time, when I was in my rollicking years, we were taught to stand up to bullies. Our parents taught us to never back down from an intimidator. The minute you run from him, he will keep picking at you, until you stand up to him. Once you stop running, he will refrain from hurting you. The point is there are no winners or losers in a fist fight. My central point is you will gain his respect. Nowadays, they have seminars, school board meetings, and orientations on tormenting

another student, for no apparent reason. A bully is given a fair warning, on the first try. If he continues to do it, he will be dismissed from the school. You're in school to grow together, not alienate those around you.

What's even more alarming is an ugly fact that some students have turned on their teachers and their fellow classmates, thanks to their fears, resentments, and frustrations. Two good examples are the Jonesboro, Arkansas, and Columbine High School tragedies that occurred in the springs of 1998 and 1999, respectively. A twelve-year-old, Mitchell Johnson, and his buddy Andrew Golden stole Andrew's grandfather's high-powered rifle, went in the woods, camouflaged themselves, and opened fire on their classmates as they were leaving school. Mitchell's reason for the shooting was that his girlfriend wanted out of their relationship because she became disinterested in him. Therefore, he took this rejection seriously, went on a shooting spree, killed four of his classmates and a schoolteacher, thirty-two-year old Shannon Wright, and injured ten other students, before finally being subdued by local authorities.

On another occasion, in a remote town named Littleton, Colorado, in the spring of 1999, two teenagers, Eric Harris and Dylan Klebald, committed perhaps the deadliest school shooting in the history of high schools. Both went into the school's cafeteria, opened fire on everyone, brutally murdered fourteen, and injured a lot more before turning their weapons on themselves. To this very day, no one will ever know what sparked them to commit such a heinous crime on the innocent students. One should a vital point to stop and smell the roses along the way. At the end of the day, nothing is gained by bullying. At the end of the school calendar year, both persons will part ways, perhaps never seeing each other again.

Be honest and fair with yourself. Are you in school to bully someone because of your personal differences or are you there to help yourself progress in your learning? You have to make that conscientious choice. It is extremely difficult to get everybody on the same page to reach a common goal. You have students with different backgrounds and upbringings to take into account. Why some students act out and behave in an irrational manner, sometimes, is still an unanswerable question to this very day. This is a growing concern that is spreading its ugly mark around the country. And this too is very problematic.

3. **Jobs.** I can only think of one place where more and more problems occur daily. And that is in the job market. It begins with the employer-employee relationship. Where would you find an organization where most employees are happy and content with their line of work? There may be in some cases, yes, but in other cases, no. To further elaborate on the latter, most of the time, we have to take positions within these companies we would not, otherwise, desire. But you have to do something to receive a paycheck and have a roof over your head. It can be frustrating and tedious when you have a particular boss who is strict and demanding or when you have a specific co-worker who works against you, rather than along with you. This can result in dissension and a turnover rate that is high. It wouldn't be easy to get the task done, based on the grounds that every employee's line of thinking is different. Moreover, some bosses might play a nasty game of politics or nepotism with certain workers. They have their chosen ones, the ones who benefit from the successes of the company, and they have the ones who

remain stagnant. In this respect, the street runs both ways. Sometimes, a particular hireling might have shot himself in the foot. By this, I mean he knew his firm's rules and regulations well. He, probably, thought he was above the law, doing certain things that go against his firm's policies. It resulted in him being dismissed, because of his inappropriate behavior. However, bosses do have the authority to replace those they may feel unsuitable or are not qualified to handle the work order.

Moreover, managements and unions do not always see eye to eye on certain issues. Sometimes, union workers may feel that they are not getting enough satisfaction from the upper brass. For instance, there might not be enough pay raises, inadequate fringe benefits, poor working conditions, unfair health benefits, lousy retirement plans, and so on. Some may feel they're making a maximum amount of performing at their minimum level with very little incentives in return. This could lead to a strike in the workforce as angry protestors protest their rights for fair working conditions. On the other side of the coin, the management may feel that if their workers become dissatisfied and do not produce adequately, then they have the upper hand to wipe the slate clean and begin with a new crew of workers. Management may feel their ideas are far better that the disgruntled workers in getting the work done with a minimum amount of effort. For example, automation's chief task is knocking manual labor out of business at a very high rate and performing tasks in an allotted amount of time. For instance, if projects were done by hand, it would take an estimated eight hours to put the finishing touches on it. With automation, it could cut the time spent doing a job almost in half. This is an issue that needs to be address.

4. **Churches.** Lastly, your desired place of worship is not exactly a paradise. A church is supposedly a place where we are forgiven of our transgressions. It should be, but it isn't. Like a management and a union not going hand in hand, in the preceding paragraph, well, some pastors may not always sit well with members of a specific church. The tactics that they use to lure members to their chapel may be obsolete or ungainly. Every new member has their perspective about how to help the church advance in society. According to the membership of that particular house of worship, the response could be fifty-fifty. There may be some who are in favor of his views and some who oppose it. Case in point, if a congregation calls in a new minister to preach, it depends on his nature of him. Like working for certain companies, does his personality match the church? Churches are run like other businesses. Some may want a minister who is conservative. Some places are not ready to accept a social change from within. They may feel that their temple is progressing at a moderate rate. Therefore, they would choose to remain stagnant in their approach. On the other hand, some would welcome a clergyman who readily accepts changes. Such a move may have to be implemented from within, thus, enabling that unique tabernacle to keep up with other chapels in advancing their program.

What's even more startling is that now you have female ministers. I'm not here to discuss the politics of this, get into a heated debate, or denigrate this fact. But this is something new presented to the church, and it poses some intriguing questions that may be open for debate. Some church officials are extremely one-sided in their viewpoints. They would ask you where in the Bible that God has called upon a lady to preach his gospel. This new problem would not coincide at all with a lot of church people. By and large, it can be a moot point. On the other side of the coin, there are many who are flexible with their opinions, beliefs, and theories, proclaiming it's all right to let a lady preach to her congregation. Again, many would argue that God does not prohibit anyone to preach. It is evident that churches or synagogues, like people, have their weaknesses too. That is why I am quite sure you have your monthly church meetings to iron out the wrinkles and help it operate on a smoother scale. It's like being on a job for a certain amount of time. You will be critiqued, evaluated, and reevaluated on your work performance. This will result in the company deciding whether to keep you on board or terminate you. The same point can be made about churches selecting preachers based on his ideas and ideals. He may be retained or let go if the people feel that the church is not headed in the right direction. Churches and people have always been feuding about what is morally right or not. Many have been feuding since the medieval days of Europe. Some are versatile in their way of thinking, thus accepting change as it comes. Yet others would resist these changes to the third degree.

A major problem with churches is not being on the same page with others over their religious beliefs. Churches have always been feuding among themselves over whose belief is right. For instance, when Christianity was on the rise, a group called the Crusaders went to Jerusalem, known as the Holy Land, and freed those people from the Muslim faith. A good majority of the Europeans were put to death in their quest for freeing those who disagreed with the Islamic faith. The Roman Catholics argued over what is celibacy or non-celibacy. This resulted in people being massacred or put out of the church. For example, if one was to ask to do away with his wife and he refused, then it was considered a faux pas, and it would have caused a religious strife. Some would argue that the three wise shepherds were not near Jerusalem when Christ was born. They were in a migratory state. This puzzle resulted in a heated debate, with many religious leaders arguing their cause to the bitter end. Better yet, at around 1692, when the Spaniards took control of the New World, they imposed their religious morals on those who were taken into captivity in such countries like Mexico and Peru. Those who disagreed with them were given very little chance of explaining their beliefs. Either they had to comply with the Spaniards or immediate persecution was passed upon them. Lastly, compelling arguments have sprung up over whether Christ was born on December 26 or December 25. Many African-Americans would argue that he was born on the latter. There have even been parades celebrating his birth the day after Christmas, supporting the fact that Kwanzaa is the true meaning of Christmas. Kwanzaa, created by Doctor Maulana Karenga in1966, is a celebration for people of African descent. It means "first hits" in their native language of Swahili. It is celebrated from December 26 to January 1. There are seven principles of Kwanzaa, one for each day. To represent each day, seven candles are used for the principle—one black, three red, and three green. They were designed for the children and the future.

These four basic puzzles, which are presented before us, can either mold or melt us. They help shape us as the human beings we are today. And how we look upon them is a call we have to make. If we stumble before them, then we have enabled them to defeat our purpose in trying to sustain a more salubrious lifestyle. We will never reap the benefits of greatness because we gave in too easily and let them dictate us. That's like saying someone has taken advantage of your good nature for their well-being. And they've taken it to the point where we stand there and do nothing about it. Your unique conundrums have gotten the best of you. But if you stick with them until the bitter end and tackle them head on, then you have learned to master the art of tackling problems. We can use each problem as a building block to allow us to grow to the next plateau in life. And from that juncture, you move on with your life. And to further put things in its proper perspective, the only obstacle standing between you and your difficulty is you.

These next three examples will give you a panoramic view of how to tackle your problems creatively and successfully. They will help you grow and mature to assist you in dealing with your daily difficulties. We begin with a judge, a union president, and a college program director—but first, the courtroom. Every courtroom that we know of has its fair share of problems as well. Every courtroom—be they criminal, civil, small claims, administrative, or child support—are here to assist us if problems get out of hand and is too big to resolve. All courtrooms are centered to help one keep his problems under control, instead of taking matters into their own hand. The characters that make up these courtrooms are judges, lawyers, jurors, and clients. Judges are there to uphold the laws and to prove if one is innocent or guilty, depending on their circumstances. The reason why we have these courtroom settings is to present both sides of the argument before coming to a fair verdict. Whichever party has a strong, valid supporting argument will be declared the unanimous winner. It is no easy task for judges to come to a fair analysis as to who was right and who wasn't. By the same token, they have a moral right to uphold the laws of this land. Let us take the case of the latter—child custody.

Judge Lisette Harris, a Philadelphia native, deals with her daily problems on a case-to-case basis. It depends on what they are. She listens to her clients' conundrum carefully and intently. She allows them to talk and be heard. Her most important task is to be fair and objective to the needs of others. She wants people to explain themselves thoroughly. Her most challenging thing is to apply the law, weigh in all the facts, and make sure she does not become too emotionally involved in any of her clients' affairs. Judge Harris feels you can become too emotional because you are dealing with everybody's personal situations. Her biggest challenge is to make sure she doesn't invest too much of her own energy. There are rewards and repercussions from her clients problems. She likes dealing with children, and when they leave, they feel certain she has done something to help them out. In terms of repercussions, any time you make decisions when you are dealing with family situations, you come in with two people, who are not in agreement, presented before the judge. That makes one person happy and the other one bitter. The repercussion is that not everybody is going to love her based on her decision. Moreover, when people leave her courtroom, they are satisfied that they have been heard but not satisfied with the results. Everybody is not going to get what he or she wants. Everybody is not always a winner when you are dealing with child custody. A child or children may become involved. Only one is going to get them. Judge Lisette Harris feels she's done what is in the best of interest of her children when they part her chambers.

Joseph Hill was president of a powerful union in Philadelphia, local 1291, for twelve years on the waterfront. One of his most trying problems was in 1987. When hiring union workers, there were no objective criteria. In short, there was no seniority. Foremen and bosses would hire any which way they chose. Some jobs would come through the hiring center. And some workers were hired off the corners, taking jobs from union men. This was first and foremost to put objective criteria, which was seniority.

The other thing was that there was plenty of work between the ports of Philadelphia and Wilmington, Delaware. Most of that work did not reach some of the union men. Therefore, Joe had to push for a craft interchange so that all union personnel would be privileged to work before any other nonunion personnel or less senior personnel. It was very challenging due to politics and the makeup of the local unions, as well as the rest of the union. Politics made way for nepotism and favoritism. People hired whoever they wanted to hire. Most of the other union officials disagreed due to the balance of political pressure and possibly losing votes, resulting in political suicide. Through it all, Joe learned that politics can run strange, and sometimes the people do not benefit from it, if you add the knife through all of that politics.

Yumy Odom, a program director at Philadelphia's Temple University, heads a program called PASCEP (Pan-African Studies Community Education Program). They offer around eighty-five different classes open to anybody in the community and other surrounding colleges. People as far as New York and Maryland come to these classes to participate in this program. Classes are held four times a week. However, one of his chief concerns is funding. Only two people are currently on his staff, but there are eighty volunteer faculty members. Ten of them are office workers. It is the one with the most outreach activities and the most impactful out of any of Temple's community programs. But there is a need for more staff. They have an effective curriculum. Work is performed. The staffing is linked to finance which is the most important piece to the puzzle. This is the most challenging problem in his administration by far. And his staff is limited. Yumy works out of his office seven days a week, from seven in the morning to ten in the evening. It may be hard work, but he feels it is a mission to get things done. Where some people have jobs, Yumy sees it as a job field. And there are rewards that come with this territory. He gets to see people learn, making him feel upright. A major piece is having a space for people to volunteer.

Also, two thousand students come here every semester. One area of concern is to have some folks have some stick-to attending classes. At around the fourth or fifth week, when it rains or snows, people stop coming to classes. Moreover, people don't call to inform him if they are coming or not. People have to understand that you cannot let the inclement weather hinder you from coming and mess up your whole class. Because there is one incident, the students will not come back at all. Yumy feels that by using his problems as a learning tree, people should be more organized. And that is why the curriculum works so well. He is well prepared and believes that others could look up to him as an example. He brought this concept to the program and feels that because there are so many different outreaches and dynamics here, the major piece is about organization and having many people support you. In his department, he has the support of his co-workers over the volunteers, staff volunteers, volunteer's registrar, volunteer people doing data entry, and volunteer night managers. Yumy strongly feels that if they were not there, he wouldn't be alive. Literally, he feels he would be working to death or he would have to cut back considerably, retrograding to 1985 standards. This industrious person feels most justified that his people have learned from him on how to master their problems. He receives great reviews from evaluations. Some of the judges have sent him letters, thanking PASCEP for GEDs. For instance, a lady judge at one time had thought about giving up. But she kept PASCEP in mind, and then she decided to stay with it, and she received her GED. Yumy receives an abundance of thank-you from so many people. His other main issue is there is no way for them to track others without his staff, because tracking people down is a whole new job. Over the past thirty-one years, probably about one hundred thousand people have come through his door, literally. Between the faculty and the students, how do you track what they are doing? Although he knows persons in the public eye who attended PASCEP, Yumy feels that his staff can see them. But then, they are basic citizens who are doing great things. Their starts came from PASCEP. PASCEP has enabled those individuals to go beyond their means Yumy Odom and his fellow workers were hoping to obtain funds from any college liberal arts program or any incoming president to keep his syllabus prospering.

As you can see, these fine individuals have mastered the art of overcoming any problem, learning from it, analyzing it from every possible angle, and moving on. They didn't let their conundrums stand in the way of achieving greatness. They stuck with it until it became routine and accepted it as part of their agenda.

If someone has a few issues with you or gives you a dirty look, more than likely you would pull him aside and ask him, "What's your problem?" or "Do you have a problem with me?" Clearly, there may be some personal issues at stake. These are just minor flaws compared to your daily ones, in which you have social contacts. At any rate, whatever problem you're associated with, big or small, relevant or irrelevant, it plays a significant role in your life. You were dealt with a different query for a number of reasons. Problems not only mold us into the people we are, but they also have a purpose in life. They prepare us for the harsh, cruel world that is ready not to welcome us with open arms. For instance, if a world crisis were to happen, like the Cuban Missile Crisis or the 911 tragedy, then we should stand up, confront them, and, eventually come to the right solution. That's equivalent to standing up to a schoolyard bully. Never cower from your personal problems. Stay with it and solve them to the best of your ability. You don't have to go around and push your panic buttons and lose your sanity. Learn from each one so you can move to the next phase in your life. There may be someone who doesn't know how to confront theirs successfully. By all accounts, be their mentor and lend them a helping hand so they can get the ball rolling. And do not think for one second that there is someone who doesn't have a specific problem to handle, because there is. It may very well be that they just know how to tackle it and keep themselves together much better than you do.

In any case, stay with yours until you come across the right formula that will do wonders for you. In finding yours, be patient until an idea or answer is suitable. They don't always come in a twinkle of an eyelash, but they will come when the need arises. A millionaire may have the luxuries to allow him to enjoy the material things in life. However, he still has one dilemma. Every morning he awakes, he has to make sure that there are no con artists or money cheaters that will try to swindle him out of his earnings. He or she has to stay on top of things, and make sure his financial earnings are not lost. And this can be a tedious lifestyle to deal with. Whatever the case, it is a serious problem to consider. Likewise, one who is rather poor does have some issues to think about. One may be at the bottom of the barrel, trying very hard to climb out of his hole to a more convenient lifestyle. If he continues to pursue with all his efforts, he will come across a remedy that will get him back on the right track. In the meantime, his problems should not dictate him in any way possible. He or she must learn from their drawbacks and convert their liabilities into assets. Thus, they will progress to the next plateau in life. So you have a litany of problems to solve, right? By all means, run to it, not away from it.

Rule 4: *Problems can be either a stumbling block or a stepping stone to success. It's a matter of how we deal with them.*

FIVE
BE NICE, NOT NASTY

It costs you nothing to be nice at all. By being polite and friendly, it gives one an inner peace and satisfaction. In addition, you give and you get respect, you make friends easily, and you travel a long way in life. Inside of your body, you release a hormone called serotonin, which enables you to be courteous. It would suit you to be nice because when you need a specific favor from someone, you are on your best behavior to win over that person. And if you see a specific job that interests you, then by all accounts, you had better be polite and considerate to that employer to get your foot in the door. So why can't we pay homage to those around us?

Becoming nasty and inconsiderate costs you a great deal of everything. You lose your friends, your acquaintances, your self-worth, your self-respect, and a great deal more. People become alienated, lose interest, and disassociate themselves from you. You walk a lonely road your whole life. Becoming crude and mean gives one a negative reputation, thus creating an atmosphere of isolation. Sometimes, being mean for no apparent reason at all may lead to, in some instances, domestic violence. No one should ever choose this path in life just to get their point across to others or to try to win over to one's way of thinking. You are hurting yourself in a number of ways by becoming vile and unpleasant. In short, you dig a deep hole for yourself to climb out of. Moreover, it is a known fact that people forget what good you've done for them. Seldom do they forget the bad that you do.

In my first job experience, fresh out of college, I took a sales job, selling shoes over the counter. In my four weeks of intensive training, the instructor emphasized politeness and respectfulness to the public. We've mastered the fundamental techniques of endorsing our products to consumers. Of course, we had to practice kindliness and patience to meet our monthly sales quotas. We were taught that anytime you work with the public, you are dealing with all kinds of personalities. And they can range from being too passive to overly aggressive. The tactics that we employed proved to be quite successful in maintaining our jobs.

Being polite to your fellow man will build up your character, self-esteem, and self-respect. People will ingratiate themselves around you. You make others feel like there is something special or important about them. It is a faux pas to treat others like dirt because of your personal differences and varying opinions. People growing up in the old South valued the notion that politeness and respect are the essential ingredients in making it in this dogmatic world. And they had a saying, which says, "You can catch more flies with honey than you can with vinegar." To put it bluntly, niceness will always conquer rudeness and nastiness because it has a stronger impact in life than all of these negative characteristics. Becoming friendly will take you places that almost everyone can only dream of. However, being wicked will demote you to a nonentity. Ultimately, you wind up going around in circles right back to square one. And you'll never know what the future had in store for you due to the fact that no one would offer their help to you. Someday, you may need a big favor from that someone to whom you were an ingrate. Perhaps, you burned bridges between you and him or her. Depending on that individual, some may have decided against rebuilding burned bridges, thus, moving down a new road in society. No one wants to get struck by lightning twice. That is why it is imperative to offer kindness and tokens of appreciation to those whom you make daily contact with. Let me repeat one more time in italic words what I said earlier in this paragraph on being nice: *You can catch more flies with honey than you can with vinegar.* This old proverb should forever stick out in the annuals of history until you become extinct.

A native African once told me that it was a necessity to respect their elders and always do right, no matter what their circumstances were, while growing up in Mica, Africa. For instance, if an elder saw a young person doing something morally wrong or headed in the wrong direction, then it was his responsibility to rectify that child for their irrational behavior. Despite that child not being their biological one, he would spank that child, and then, report their wrongdoings to their parents. In the present time, if someone noticed an infant doing something wrong down the street from him, then he would whip him to correct his faults and weaknesses until his original parents got hold of him. Maybe these tactics would not coincide with us because our concept of bringing someone up is worlds apart from another individual's way. Moreover, our customs and traditions are not same as they are over in Mica, West Africa.

Don't be cruel or coldhearted because you are baffled and frustrated from being unable to obtain your long-sought-after desires. There are many other avenues to take to see your results. Unfortunately, nastiness won't cut it. Use a little protocol and diplomacy in establishing a healthy, happy, and harmonious relationship among your peers. It can help, not hurt. Never use a mean tactic to bully another person around just to win someone over to your side of the story. Always use prudent judgment in making things right for the next fellow you have contact with. Put yourself in the other person's shoes. If someone were to be nasty to you, then how would that make you feel? It would make you feel guilty and inferior. You would avoid his presence to the extreme. By all means, throw that approach away. Always remember this golden rule: be nice, not nasty.

Rule 5: *Be kinder than necessary.*

SIX

A CONSISTENT CONCEPT

This chapter is a follow-up to the very first one that begins this book. I will attempt to make it as clear and concise as possible. Let me begin by saying that those students, athletes, businesspeople, politicians, entertainers, or whoever, have all gone through different phases in life. In sustaining their goals, their roads were no easy paths to take. Many times, I am quite sure they felt like quitting or going into another profession. And you may have felt like them as well. This could be due largely in part to your ups and downs. For instance, you may have experienced some physical and mental fatigue. You may have lost some interest, or became annoyed, disappointed, and dispirited with yourself. In any case, all of these ingredients come with the territory. Sometimes, mulling over these setbacks could deprive you of a proper night's rest or let negative thoughts creep into your mind. Like in the preceding chapter, the college program director, Yumy Odom, works constant hours in his administration just to right the wrongs. They range from 7:00 A.M. to 10:00 P.M. And I am quite sure he has experienced some mental drudgery and exhaustion. There is one concept that sums up everything in this opening paragraph. And this specific word is very broad. It should be forever written in your memory. It's called consistency.

Consistency is the key that unlocks all of the hidden treasures within you. Consistency will take you to unimaginative places you never thought existed. Consistency will open new avenues for you. Consistency will take you to the farthest end of this earth. Consistency will enable you to deal with any pitfalls or setbacks you encounter. And by overcoming these obstacles, you will have mastered the fundamental qualities associated with this sixty-four-dollar word in striving for greatness. They won't come at the first try, but by hanging in there, they will eventually come. By working assiduously and hard, you will come to your conclusion. A case in point is running a marathon. Consider what runners have to put themselves through just to finish a strong one. It takes a six-month grueling training regimen to prepare for this event. Both physical and mental anguish can creep into your thoughts. You ask yourself, "Is it worth it?" If things don't go right, you may experience some discouragement. The steady grinding of pounding the streets cans seem like a duty, not a hobby. Nonetheless, the successful marathoner has to practice, persevere, and have patience through it all to complete his grinding task.

Or take the case of a professional singer. One has to spend interminable hours of rehearsals to perfect his song, before he records it. His words must be properly enunciated, articulated, well-timed, and well-tuned with various keys. Moreover, one must have sound voice control from a voice coach. Singer Lauryn Hill is a witness to that. She brought her goals into fruition through practice and hard work. Like I said in the last paragraph, consistency will bring great things to the table if you stick with what you are doing. And as a result, she has received numerous rewards and Grammys, thus, helping her expand her illustrious singing career. The trick to her success was practicing a song close to a hundred times, just to get it right. One year, sold over seventeen million copies of the record. Thanks to her commitment, Lauryn prevailed.

Growing up in the sultry Texas climate, this one proud person would chop wood to earn a living for him and his family. He would chop wood from 7:00 A.M. to midnight during his childhood years. There were many times when tedium and depletion were his foes. But he persevered through all of this. To him, it may have seemed like there was no light at the end of the tunnel. But there was. Despite his hardships, determination, grit, and sweat, he never deviated from his principles. This type of consistency has earned him a chance to play professional football. He rose from adversity to prominence by chopping wood to help pay for his college expenses. He invented the infamous "chop block" he uses when he makes a solo tackle on his opponents. His name is Jeremiah Trotter, a solid middle linebacker for the Philadelphia Eagles. The honorable Leon Sullivan once said, "It's not where you've been, but it's where you're going that matters." Jeremiah Trotter is a great representation of that proverb.

Here's something to think about. Politicians never have an easy time trying to get elected to a certain position in the political arena. It's a year-round, grind-it-out job to try to win over the public's approval. Amid the false reports, negative advertisements, and knife-in-the-back tactics they use on each other, they have to weather the storm through all of these letdowns to gain a desirable position that best suits them. Their campaign trails are long, challenging, and hard. Their campaign money from fund-raising events has to be put to proper use. Some of these contestants may call it quits after a few tries but others will stick it out to the bitter end, no matter what the circumstances are. Each legislator's meaning of consistency is different from the rivals. The paths they take will, ultimately, determine if they succeed or falter. One thing that is certain is that they must believe in honesty.

A state representative, Larry Curry, is an eyewitness to this thinking. It takes money for any politician to win over his adversary. He has to stay focused. Despite overcoming hardships, challenges, disappointments, or the overwhelming odds against him, Larry stuck to his guns and won his seat. And his one advice he would pass on to anyone in their endeavors is to remain honest. Larry feels that in this respect, honesty is the best policy. Larry believes that one should always stay the course in sustaining one's accomplishment. Always believe in hard work, integrity, and consistency.

Doing college work is, by no means, an easy task to master, especially, if you want to pursue a post–high school education. Everyone has a time frame within themselves as to when they will maintain their degrees. Some are destined to graduate ahead of schedule. Some are bound to graduate on schedule. Others are prone to graduate later than their set time limits. There is no exact time as to when you are expected to complete your degree. The crux of my argument is those that don't always graduate as anticipated may have to study somewhat harder than others to earn their right to happiness. The steady grinding hours of studying to fulfill your dreams can be brutal, agonizing, and disturbing to the mind, body, and soul. Many days and nights, you may feel it is of no use to obtain a worthwhile degree. You ask yourself, "Was all this studying and mental discipline worth it?" If you do, then you really haven't mastered your dreams or aspirations that you set for your career. Never give in to negativity, doubtfulness, or despair because you didn't make it at the first try. There's always a second chance to triumph over your failures and difficulties.

I did not complete my degree as expected within the four-year plan. Upon entering my freshman year, I was unsure as to what area of interest I want to be practicing for the rest of my life. Some students find themselves at a very early age. Others find themselves at a later one. Mine was the latter. All of these interests were like a wide—open spectrum to choose from. My job was to narrow it down and choose a specific area that best suited me. As a young introvert, I had to learn through trial and error that even though I received high marks for my work, I had to take my studies to a whole new level. Moreover, I didn't want to play "catch-up" in my studies, because it is difficult to keep pace with the instructors when you get behind. Such was my intent, if I was to graduate, move on, and give someone else a chance to learn.

Speaking of learning, on another venture, I wanted to share this amazing story with you from one of my college buddies, Miss J—— S——. The reason is because it may be unique, but it is newsworthy and inspirational. And this is what she told me. She attended a very small law school. In her first year, she noticed there was only one black student in the entire school. When she arrived for her second year, she went to use the school's public phone, which was situated near the law-school bulletin board. As she was waiting for her call to go through, she started reading a newspaper article tacked on the board. It announced the arrival of a new African-American woman from the South. She had arrived with only two dollars in her pocket, unlike some of the other students from wealthier families, who drove in as freshmen with brand new cars given to them by their parents; sometimes when they graduated, they would receive another new car. J—— didn't have a great deal of money herself. She was one of a few students who paid their way entirely by themselves. But as she was reading the article, a black woman suddenly appeared right beside her. She exclaimed, "You must be the woman in this article." She assured J—— that she was and J—— introduced herself. The two struck up an interesting conversation, and at the end, J—— said to her, "If you need any help, be sure and give me a call." A few days later, she did call and asked for help in writing her first term paper.

J—— was fortunate to have a good education. She took it very seriously and studied more than anyone she knew. But her new friend didn't have the same opportunities as she. J—— was a humanitarian. She wanted to help in any way, shape, or form possible. Get this! It took them fourteen straight hours—*fourteen straight hours!*—to wade through the first page of her paper. J—— had to show her all of the fundamentals and techniques of writing a paper. Furthermore, to say that she felt badly for her would be an understatement. She could not construct a simple sentence. They worked together, day after day, week after week, and month after month. She will admit that at the beginning, she never imagined that she would ever get through law school and graduate. But they worked very hard and never gave up. And it did take an incredible amount of dedication and effort. But she persevered. And the weeks turned into months and the months turned into years. When she graduated, J—— was right there to celebrate with her. A few years later, the law school hired her back to become its dean of diversity. She subsequently told J—— that she attributes all of her professional success to her. However, J—— knew better. Her friend is the perfect illustration of the success that one can obtain when he or she sets her mind on a goal, even a lofty one. Goals, most certainly, are attainable with dedication, ambition, hard work, and perhaps a little good fortune thrown in. Such was the element of surprise in her friend's case.

Here's another riveting story I heard some years ago from a radio interview. It inspired me to do some research off the internet of this underappreciated American. He was born the grandson of a slave in a log cabin in Marshall, Texas, January 18, 1898. When he was eight years old, he began working to help support his family. He never learned to read or write. He survived a decade of hard work by chopping wood, working in a saw mill, and building levees on the mighty Mississippi River with the help of a mule. He laid ties for some of the first railroads in East Texas. He had to sweep floors, clean for whites, and for a majority of his working life—twenty-five years—ran the machines that pasteurized milk at Oak Farms Dairy. While working at Oaks Farms, he lost a golden opportunity for a chance at a promotion, due to one factor—he could not sign his name. Instead, he signed it with an "X." For the majority of his life, he had to endure the hostile mistreatment and segregation the South heaped upon black people. He continued to deal with racism all of his life.

Then at ninety-eight years old, it hit him like lightning. He attended school. On a winter day in 1996, a teacher by the name of Carl Henry was filling in for another teacher in an adult basic literacy class when he walked in. Henry had retired from the Dallas school system after thirty-three years as an educator. Henry wanted to know if this stranger knew the alphabet. A "no" was his reply. Over the weeks, months, and years that followed, Henry taught him to read.

In 1998, another elementary school teacher, Richard Glaubman, read an article about a Texas man who learned how to read and write. He became inspired and interested. He made an arrangement to meet him. Something good always comes out of a bad situation (as I will elaborate on in one of my later chapters) because the two men eventually wrote an award-winning book titled *Life Is So Good*. And one of the authors who finally learned how to read and write after a century was George Dawson. Dawson was 103 years old when his book was published. This book tells of Dawson's remarkable life through his eyes and experiences and tells of his burning desire to become literate. Glaubman has appeared on many programs, such as *CBS News Sunday Morning* and *Good Morning, America*. Dawson's book has had rave reviews from magazines like the *New York Times, Christian Science Monitor, USA Today,* and the *Washington Post.* In addition, it was chosen for the Book of the Month Club, and other awards followed.

It was a philosophy from his father that inspired George Dawson to write this book. Despite their hardships, George tells how he and his father overcame many obstacles and saw the richness in life. He passed this theory on to his children. Throughout his story, Dawson has left us with an inspiring message that should be indelibly written on your memory: "Life is so good. I do believe it's getting better." Dawson is proof positive to that testimony. And in a long chain of unheralded successful people, he is a wonderful example of what consistency will do for you.

Without any uniform standard, you would have no specific aim in life, in any area of interest that strikes you. Your beliefs, ambitions, dreams, and desires are the unquestionable components that will see you through the final stages of your life's incredible journey to obtain greatness. Your goals, be they long or short range, lofty or lowly, tangible or intangible, will determine how well you define success. Nothing, which is worth achieving within its chance, will happen overnight. It will come with time, patience, and experience. Success is not always measured in monetary rewards or in popularity but how well you, assiduously, plug away at something that you may be minutes away from grasping. There is no clear-cut or universal solution for prosperity. Everybody's idea of happiness is miles apart different from their fellow human being. Before closing out this section, I would like to leave you with a small verse I've written on consistency. It says:

> To persevere in our paths, through the winds of time, amid our setbacks, our mishaps, our despairs, a resistant.
>
> From the very first step to the very last we endure, gives a new meaning on being consistent.

A gifted musician rehearsed countless hours to perfect her songs. A football player went to any extremes with his guts and sweat by hacking wood for a living. And as a result of that, his guts and sweat are poured out on the grid iron. A statesman warded off dishonesty by remaining honest in a fight for his seat. And two illiterates from the South had high hopes for learning the English language, despite their ages. Each of these people controlled their own destinies within their own rights by believing in the conception of consistency. They all managed to turn their liabilities into assets. Each of the individuals that I've highlighted in this section goes without questioning their potential for reaching their triumphs. They were high-spirited and possessed plenty of zest to proceed to another chapter in their lives. Like sports teams taking their level of intensity to a whole new plateau, so did these pioneers take their level of consistency to another level. Again, George Dawson comes to mind as a fine example. In his book, he had many short sayings, which apply to our own daily needs. One of them says, "People worry too much. Life is good just the way it is." Change what you can and leave the rest as is.

Rule 6: *Without consistency there is no moral strength.* —*Owen.*

SEVEN

OVERCOMING VERBAL ABUSE

There is no antidote for it. There is no magic formula to make it do wonders for anyone. Its presence is inescapable. Depending on how you view it, it can either make or break you. Whatever field of interest you pursue, it will be your kissing cousin for the entirety of your life. We eat, sleep, drink, breathe, and study its side effects. Even in our activities, we are prone to its welcoming arms. It lingers in our schools, houses, churches, jobs, clubs, and even in our sophisticated fraternal organizations, from colleges, universities, or just in general. It is a known fact that, while we are in existence, people will condemn us for actions and deeds. In death, they extol you and start to see things from your perspective No one, regardless of their ethnicity, ages, rank, or status, big or small, important or not, can ever hide from its repercussions.

Do your words heal or hurt? The reason I ask is because someone may be in desperate need of a helping hand. They may have hit rock bottom because of their circumstance. They may not know how to climb out of their predicament. And your words can be a healing balm to them, enabling them to get back into the swing of things. Everyone in life has their down days, but that does not mean we should go around reacting to another person in a negative way, just to get them on the same page we are on. Your mind is a powerful tool, and it can play its little tricks on you. It may make you feel you are in control of everything you encounter. You can do no wrong. And everyone is not that strong-minded to be able to ward off impolite, discouraging words. It is unwise to say things to those we don't even know a lick about. We don't know for sure if one may feed off your criticism the way we want them to. If we don't properly apply our comments, then we could alienate those with whom we come in contact on a daily basis. This is a surefire way of making enemies.

Verbal abuse is here to stay, whether we accept it or not. There are plenty of times that we have to take a number of things in stride we don't want to. And unfortunately, this abusive scolding from someone else's mouth is one of them. The diatribe we thrust upon each other diurnally could result in us becoming too emotionally involved with what others around us are doing or saying that is not in cahoots with our standard of living. Our egos are insulted, our feelings are hurt, and our pride is destroyed. All of this negativity results in our crucifying one another. It makes no difference whether one likes or dislikes whomever. If you are extremely busy, living a sedentary life, or perhaps an invalid, criticism will find you. The majority of this section is about dealing with or overcoming another's caustic comments. Unfortunately, we have to learn and grow from its aftereffects. Some know how to properly apply their techniques on others. Perhaps, they use some protocol or are diplomatic in their usage to get their points across. We must learn how to master these unwanted situations with delicacy and protocol because of acrimonious remarks from different tongues. You are best suited to study the character of a person beforehand, before attempting to inject your daily dosage of unkind words at another. You will never know how that person will respond to your harsh words.

The Washington, Du Bois, and Garvey Factor

Not only does verbal abuse come from all walks of life, but it also comes from every aspect of it as well. Three well-known dignitaries experienced one another's vitriolic comments. They were professionals in their line of work, but they had to overcome many scurrilous remarks from each other's mouths. Their names were Booker T. Washington, William Edward Burghart Du Bois, and Marcus Mosiah Garvey. All three civil rights activists had some harsh words for each other, while fulfilling their sense of purpose. And all of this drama unfolded in the year the great Frederick Douglass died, in 1895. And it continued for many, many years. Their strong dislike for one another expanded out into the open public. These men were extremely gifted and brilliant beyond their years and recognition for their fight for equality and justice for blacks. To further underscore what I'm saying is Du Bois took on two of his fiercest rivals in trying to win them over to his way of thinking. For Du Bois and Washington, their rivalry was tense but friendly. As for Du Bois and Garvey, it was tense and bitter. In some cases, it became personal. First, we begin with the feud concerning Du Bois and Washington.

Du Bois and Washington

Politics, like football, has taken a whole new turn, nowadays. It has stepped up its game to another level. Back at the turn of the twentieth century, two unheralded politicians often clashed over their issues of improving the living conditions for blacks. They were Booker T. Washington and W. E. B. Du Bois. Their debates over equality and fairness for blacks were rather long and intense. Washington was born into slavery himself. He grew up on the notion that blacks could improve their conditions through an industrial education. To Washington, progress meant industry. He felt blacks could elevate themselves through manual labor. He recommended doing for white people what they could not do for themselves: remove the Negro from national politics and political talk. Rather than try to alter the course of history somewhat, make the best of a bad situation and move on, he theorized. Washington had a myriad of wealthy whites and his college, Tuskegee Institute, who backed him up. All of these big-name people needed cheap workers for their labor. The white laborers and the poor whites looked at blacks as their foes, not their allies. Even his associates, made up of martinets and disciplinarians, wanted blacks to have everything second class in nature. But his vision failed. Segregation produced more segregation.

Du Bois's story is of a new nature. Du Bois reasoned that improvement of life for blacks begins with education as its firm foundation. He believed blacks must educate blacks. In order for Negroes to compete on the level of other races and cultures, education was a must. Moreover, he believed that schools, churches, colleges, and universities played an integral part in the quality of Negro lives. And the only way to do this was to educate blacks on how slavery got started in Africa and her refusal to accept slavery. Furthermore, Du Bois was dead set against Washington and his policies, which were like using drill sergeants to segregate the races. Instead, his motivation was for teachers and students to have a "long family relationship." However, some of his visions, like his adversaries, Booker T. failed because many felt he was overtaken with selfishness and egoism. Just as many black leaders opposed Washington, many of them opposed Du Bois as well. The feeling was fifty-fifty.

The drama between Du Bois and Washington didn't end there. At the 1895 Atlanta Exposition, Washington was asked to deliver his address at the international affair. He gave a brilliant, dazzling speech on improving race relations with Southern blacks and whites. However, Du Bois saw it differently. He sharply criticized his rival when Washington used a line in his speech, calling for everyone to "cast down your bucket where you are." He felt that this form of compromise would not equal the white man's society. Instead, it would lead to a separate black society. Du Bois stressed that blacks champion their rights and privileges in an already-free society. Many white politicians extolled Washington for his stupefying speech. But many black leaders, especially around the country, opposed him, including black clergymen.

He received numerous letters of condemnation from what was said. Some parents even ceased sending their children to his institution. But Washington stood firm in his concept. Even Du Bois ripped him apart for his comments. However, a few days later, he sent Washington a letter of apology. Both men put aside their differences and proceeded to get on with their works.

Du Bois and Garvey

The whole situation with Du Bois and Gamey grew nasty and ugly. The heated debate between the two over the issues of black American lives was very bitter. It was so bitter that it became personal, in some instances. Garvey's roots trace back to Jamaica. Later on, he relocated to New York City and spent the remainder of his life there. But his feud with Du Bois began while Du Bois was vacationing in Jamaica. Du Bois said that the race problem in Jamaica was over. Garvey heard his comments and was angry about it. In 1919, Garvey visited New York and came to the NAACP (National Association for the Advancement of Colored People) headquarters. But the rift between the two men would only widen. Garvey found out that most of the workers were white. This infuriated him even more, more to the point where he called the NAACP the "National Association for the Advancement of Certain People" meaning the black middle class and their white friends, not for blacks as a whole. Again, in 1920, Garvey's remarks were the first open breach to the public. It was learned that Du Bois attended one of their meetings. And Garvey later said, "If Du bois were a new Negro working for the freedom of his race, we would have been glad to know he was there. When we think of big Negroes, we do not think of him."

Du Bois, on the other hand, criticized the UNIA (United Negro Improvement Association) economics programs without naming names. He foresaw what Garvey's intentions were. Garvey wanted a black society all to its own. Du Bois felt that integration was a key ingredient to improving the quality of black life. And he firmly believed that the backing of black institutions would be a valuable asset in the development of the black race in an already-mixed society. He refuted Garvey's tactics and demeanor. For instance, it was learned that Garvey was interested in the shipping business. But he didn't have sound financial statements to back him up. Moreover, his subordinates were inadequately trained to operate ships. He came under attack from Du Bois. Here is what Du Bois had to say about his rival: "He is a sincere, hardworking idealist, but he is also a stubborn, domineering leader of the mass. He has worthy, industrial, and commercial schemes, but he is an inexperienced businessman ... his methods are bombastic, wasteful, illogical and ineffective, and almost illegal ..."

Meanwhile, here are Garvey's recriminations on Du Bois: "As we study the personality of Du Bois, we find that he only appreciates one type of man. And that is the cultured, redefined type, which lingers around universities and pink-tea affairs. Dr. Du Bois cannot appraise at their face value ... he could not, thus far, become the popular leader of the masses of his own race ..." For many incoming years, the battle from both sides persisted, with neither one giving in to another's methods. Their animosity and open criticism got to the point where it almost resulted in character assassination from both parties. It was apparent that the feuding two left a bitter taste in each other's mouths. Despite their course of action, all three civil rights activists felt justified in bringing about a better change for blacks living in America.

Cosby's Castigation

To bring you up to date, the NAACP always holds its yearly conventions in different cities. One of them was Philadelphia. And it was in the summer of 2004. Many guest speakers and delegates convened from around the country to listen, discuss, and address various issues on improving the quality of race relations.

One notable speaker for that evening was one of Philadelphia's prodigal sons. His name was William Cosby, a popular comedian and community activist. But we all know him as Bill. Many experts and critics hail him as the "father of our country" because of his expanded education and knowledgeable experiences. On this particular night, many came out to see if he would tell jokes and titillate them. The initial focus of the group was to discuss economic injustices and the poor allocation of money to black schools. Not so on this particular night. Were they in for a rude surprise! Cosby thought otherwise. His verbal assault was on the fact that apathetic black parents and children are not putting enough emphasis on education. "Let me tell you something!" he begins. "You're dirty laundry gets out of school at two thirty in the afternoon every day. It's cursing and calling each other n———. They are walking up and down the streets." Also, Cosby said at a later meeting, "They think they're hip. They can't read or write. They're laughing and giggling, but they are going nowhere." His vitriolic comments delighted some but angered many, who felt his words were too harsh and abrasive and took away from racism and inequality.

Many delegates and other political leaders had mixed reviews about his comments. Others reasoned that his diatribe was a wake-up call to the African American community. Even the mayor himself, John Street, was an example of how others felt about the popular entertainer's comments. One side of him believed that we are to blame for our wrongdoings. He foresaw the fact that blacks were shooting each other in the foot, so to speak. Another side of him felt that racism was a liability in mainstream America, having experiencing some himself as a child growing up in his school years. Another Philadelphia icon, Congressman Chaka Fattah, agreed with the comic, but to a degree. He sensed that today's students may need better resources, but they also need to be motivated. He wondered if they lost the zeal of the civil rights era when blacks had to perform 110 percent to be considered on the same level as whites.

Mayor's Reproach

Hurricane Katrina left its devastating effects on the city of New Orleans. It may have been the worst storm ever to hit an American city in the history of this great nation of ours. Many lives were destroyed, and many neighborhoods were ravaged, especially in the black community. The hurricane cost the city billions of dollars to repair the damages and restore it back to its proper condition. Not only were many people hurt and confused about what transpired, but they were also bitter and annoyed. One of them could not help but be angry at the popular city. Of all things considered, he is a person in the public eye. His name is Ray Nagin.

Mayor Nagin lashed out at everyone in the city of New Orleans, saying that Hurricane Katrina was a sign that "God is mad at America" and at black communities. "Surely, God is mad at America. He has sent us hurricane after hurricane after hurricane, and it's destroyed and put stress on our country," he said. And the irony of it all is he said this while in observance of Martin Luther King Day. He furthered added, "Surely, he doesn't approve of us being in Iraq under false pretenses. But surely, he is upset with black America also. We are not taking care of ourselves first." He later said some more negative comments that caught everyone's attention. His aspersions drew nationwide attention. Almost every black leader, organization, and civic groups from everywhere vented their anger and dislike for the mayor for such outright remarks. Some even wanted him to resign as mayor, but he stood firm on his issues. Nagin thought about his remarks on the city, because a day later, he issued a formal apology to those who were offended by it in New Orleans and elsewhere. To agree or disagree with Nagin is a moot point. The mayor was using his candor as an alarm clock to wake them up.

The Ashanti and Tweet Factor

Like politics, sports, or whatever, the music industry, likewise, has taken on a whole new twist. In this day and age of sophisticated living, music has elevated itself to another plateau. And what's even more notable is two gifted legendary musicians were exchanging unpleasant words with each other. She has been crowned the undisputed queen of hip-hop of her generation. Ashanti is her name. And her competitor is named Tweet. We have two female recording artists exchanging words against each other. It was reported in the 2002 March edition of the magazine, *Honey*, that Tweet claims her music is soul with originality. She feels that she is more original than her recording rival. This all started with a beef with Def Jam Recordings. The company bought the majority of Ashanti's albums. She believes the sales thing might be political. But she does acknowledge that she and Ashanti are both good in their own ways. Ashanti feels somewhat different. Her argument is the recording company bought her albums to increase her sales and make them go platinum. She probably feels Tweet might be slightly jaded. Ashanti did mention that she respects Tweet for her opinion. Tweet believes she is more original than her. But Ashanti did mention the fact that she will never bow down to Tweet in any way possible. Unlike Du Bois, Washington, and Garvey, Ashanti and Tweet are friends and have love for one another's music. Despite these minor differences, many critics feel that Ashanti might be somewhat controversial in her persona because of her frankness with the public and her fans. It can best be said that the two popular singers are both talented in displaying their music to the world. Since then, the rift has long been healed between them.

Richard's Rancor

Again, let us take the case of another popular entertainer. This time, it was no singer, no musician, and no politician that went into a tirade.

It was a comedian at a nightclub spot. He was in the midst of telling jokes when two black hecklers from the audience started heckling him. The reason so was because they felt his jokes were lifeless, dry, and dull witted. Evidently, these hecklers must have pushed the wrong buttons, or he was feeling rather low at the moment. Michael Richards is his name. He started shouting racial slurs and obscenities at the two. His rancor was so great that he couldn't keep all of his hate bottled up in his system. Richards exploded on stage with so many anti-black slurs for three and a half minutes. A handful of whites got up and walked out on him because they didn't want him representing them as being disrespectful to another culture.

Richard's outrage drew bitterness and hatred from many African American legislatures, civil rights leaders and activists, community activists, church leaders, and other black organizations, protesting that he should be permanently banned from any nightclub act or television series. The radios, televisions, and newspapers gave their opinions and viewpoints on why he came across as such a moron act out in the manner he did. Words are much more piercing than a sharp knife or weapon. Physical pain is temporary. Mental pain is permanent. It can take one a lifetime to recover from such abusive remarks. For the comedian, it was a night of insults, not a night of laughs.

Old School versus New School

What's with this old school versus new school mentality? Does it really have an impact on one generation's course of action over another? Maybe in some cases, yes! But as for most cases, no! Regardless of what generation you were born in, you are always prone to criticism in all your endeavors. One lineage may be offended or take things in a different way. Again, let us take the case of the music industry. Most young people are turned on by the style and lyrics of today's music, like rap, hip-hop, reggae, disco, and Latin music. The lyrics may be long if you listen to it but also powerful and, in some cases, offensive and insulting. They are turned on by the idea that these songs are slightly longer to listen to for their taste and amusement. In this era of music, like the hip-hop, disco, or rap, it is acceptable as a new form of music. Contrariwise, yesterday's listeners prefer a more laid-back, low-key approach to music like rhythm and blues, soul, gospel, and jazz. The older music lover may perceive it as a turnoff. One may think that some of its lyrics are too long, powerful, and provocative, thus killing the effect of the song. They may think it is too boring for one's taste. The older person desires a more conservative approach to this particular brand of music, as opposed to a young person's wild and radical style for his desired form of entertainment. The older generation feels he's too conservative to change his approach. He finds it difficult to adapt to the changing times of being up on things. Thus, he is habitual in his lifestyle.

Another prime example is how we dress to impress others. There was a time when people dressed conservatively to become noticeable. In a classroom setting, we were brought up on the notion that we had to dress like we were gearing up for a job interview. And it was a taboo to let you hair grow to any length. People from a bygone era looked upon this particular fad as a clear misrepresentation of them. But for the next generation, it was welcomed with open arms. You could grow your hair and sideburns to any length you desire. The thick heels on your shoes were considered a popular trend. Thus, you created a laid-back atmosphere in your classroom or business setting. One viewed it as liberal, not conservative. A different one frowns upon things, which a new breed of people views today as in style. One may lampoon another because of his ideas, ideals, and beliefs on what he considers as traditional. But remember that the future quickly becomes the present. And the present quickly becomes the past. Another way to put it mildly is, according to the laws of time, the new school will eventually become old school. Every succeeding generation has their way of getting things done. One man's trash is another man's treasure.

Reginald Murray

On Lying

Is lying a major component of verbal abuse? Well, let's elaborate some. We don't know to this present day why people lie to themselves and on others. They probably feel that one might be "getting one over on them." The Bible does admonish us that the minute you are born in the flesh, you sin naturally. And one of the sin bins of the world is lying. On the other hand, lying can leave an ugly mark on others, which only time can mend. Sometimes, it has resulted in deaths of innocent victims. It is hard to erase something that is fallacious. Not everybody can take this form of criticism lightly. Some can dismiss it easily. But many will take falsehood very seriously because it can damage one's reputation to a large extent. The public is gullible as to what is said about others in the open. The news media, press, magazines, newspapers, television, and radio can exaggerate about comments from one individual or another. Why do we lie to others? It could be that we feel jaded over our own accomplishments. Or we feel we need to make a lasting impression on those we socialize with, making a strong impression to win them over to our way of living. Or it could be we want to make those believe more than what we are. Some will go to their extremes to impress others. It is a moral wrong to put out negatives reports on others that aren't even true.

But is lying a major component? Seemingly, I think it is. Many people's lives have been shattered, destroyed, or drastically changed in a negative way over a fabrication. Their reputations have been stigmatized to the point where sometimes libel suits are necessary against the individual or individuals who made up an outright lie to slander others reputation. And those distinct individuals, who couldn't prove otherwise, were, in some cases, sent to jail. How many times in the past have our judicial system sent people to their deaths, when, later on, they were found innocent? We would not want to see this happening to another innocent bystander. It is unwise and unjust to denigrate one's character in public or in private over a boldface, neon, and outrageous inconceivable lie. Clearly, to this present day, one will never know if one is telling the truth or a mere falsehood simply by having to eye-to- eye contact. And, of course, we do have people telling little, white lies to avoid precarious situations. For instance, we often tell a fib while dating as we try to win over someone's affection, which we consider very dear to us. We lie to get our feet in the door of certain jobs that impress us. I could go on and on with all kinds of deceitful lies, but I won't. Some more classic examples are from people in the public domain. Martha Stewart and singer, actress, rapper Li'l Kim had to pay their dues by doing some jail time because they made up untrue stories to conceal evidences. Perhaps the biggest lie of them all and one that will surely stick out in minds of millions of Americans for a number of generations to come is the Watergate scandal, involving President Richard Nixon lying to Congress, trying to cover up some tapes he used. I won't go any further on this issue. My point is to speak falsely of another's character is a no-no. One should never live on lies to avoid a seemingly difficult situation.

Years ago, a minister talked about his son, who would go around lying because he thought there was some fun in it. I cannot exactly remember what he actually said verbatim, but I do know that over the course of time, he eventually straightened up. He matured to the point where he stopped lying because he found out, that later on, the naked truth would be revealed. Something must have hit him deep down inside to change his life. One day, he approached his father, saying, "Dad, I stopped lying. I realize it's no use to keep lying." His father's reply was, "Son, you stopped your lying. But did you know that it left an ugly mark on your character? You've created some mental scars. Only time can mend them. You cannot do so yourself." Think about that! Think what these misstatements can do to another being. They can do more than just destroy one's reputation. They can leave a lasting mental tear on one to overcome for quite some time. When a child is young, he would tell a make -believe story for inexcusable behavior. He will go to any length to try and conceal the evidence to avoid any form of punishment from his parents. This may include a few spankings, not being allowed to play with his favorite toy for a while, or being sent to bed without any supper. In any case, children or adult, we make up such unwarranted untrue stories because we may feel threatened by those around us or to eschew getting ourselves in hot water. There is no justification for imposing nasty, insecure lies on each other. Truth is more potent than a concocted lie. As in every case, a lie will only back up another lie. But the truth will set you free.

On Long-Windedness

Abraham Lincoln took the long tedious train ride from Washington, D. C. to deliver his famous Gettysburg address to the eyes of the nation, concerning his issues with slavery. Thousands braved the heat and humidity to hear what the president had to say. Until he arrived, many had heard other guest speakers express their opinions and theories on how to reunite war-torn America and abolish slavery. Some spoke for as much as an hour to an hour and a half. Some spoke for nearly two hours. People were starting to lose interest. Some were growing impatient, wondering if Lincoln would ever show. When the president finally arrived, many came to life and gathered around the podium to listen. They thought that he would talk as long as the others did. But did Lincoln do that? No! He spoke for exactly two minutes—*two minutes alone!*—much to their amazement. What do you suppose Lincoln did afterward? Did he stay and mull around, sign autographs, and converse with his audience? Not at all! He immediately proceeded to see an injured friend from the war, paid his respects, and headed back on the train to Washington. Thousands of spectators, who stood around for nearly a day to see the icon, went home somewhat disappointed. They wanted more from him but got less. Such was Lincoln's persona.

A Successful Formula

On a balmy November night in Philadelphia, three weeks before the primary elections, City Councilman John F. Street, was campaigning hard to run for mayor. I was there in attendance to witness such a rally at a packed church. Other state and local officials were also in attendance to endorse him. One of those officials was a former mayor himself, W. Wilson Goode. Again, these politicians, clergymen, businessmen, or whoever, expressed their points of view in favor of Street. As for Mayor Goode, he spoke on behalf of the candidate for about a minute. According to my calculations, if I am not mistaken, seconds before he departed, he didn't fail to say, "You all don't need me to tell you what to do. You know what to do. You all have some homework to do." And what do you think he did? He said his good-byes and disappeared into the night.

On a sad note, my family and I went to our cousin's funeral. During the ceremony, we were informed to speak for two minutes to express our praise for the deceased. One of the members got up, spoke, and stretched the two minutes into an almost twelve-minute speech. And to say that she knew what she was talking about would be an exaggeration. She was repetitious and rhetorical in her eulogy. The audience became annoyed and impatient. Others wanted to express their comments so the service could proceed. Afterward, the minister got up and said that anyone else speaking would be restricted to two minutes alone.

You don't have to stretch a sentence into a ten-minute speech for others to see your point. All of this verbiage is unnecessary. The reason I say so is because a person's attention span is exactly one-sixty-fourth of an inch. If you were to speak at any public function to a strange crowd, you wouldn't want them to become bored and disinterested in what you have to say. It would be displeasing, disinterested, and disappointing to you, if they were to get up and walk out on you. You can say a lot by saying little as opposed to saying little by saying a lot. Always be considerate of another's wishes and needs whenever you give a lecture or statement in public. Be concise as much as possible. Don't beat around the bush. Never say the same things over and over because it's like beating a dead horse to death. Be exact and move on.

Is your criticism fair or unfair, justifiable or unjust? The reason I ask is because not every person have elephant's skin. Many people are sensitive to sharp criticism. Some have a difficult time rebounding from its negative effects. Your choice of words will reveal your true character by what you say and how you use them. Dealing with or overcoming one's verbal abuse is no easy matter. This verbal assault we hear constantly is another quality of life we have to encounter. You could very well be a benefactor, a malefactor, or a do-nothing person. It will still stay with you, until you become extinct. Criticism, in its rarest form, is something to learn from, not to toss aside. No one will ever know for sure if one's acerbic comments, aimed at another, are due to the fact that one may have some fish to fry. Still, we have to turn a deaf ear to those we consider to be our adversaries and keep pressing on to greater things. More importantly, when we censure others, it's a matter of when, where, and how we employ it. Humans will be humans. But does that mean we should infect every living soul with our negativity because they don't see things from our perspective? No, we shouldn't. Never let your disparaging remarks dictate how you should feel about another man's character. Sometimes, letting your true feelings be known means you may very well have burned bridges between you and that distinct individual. Above all, never let heresy, gossip, or any made-up rumors con you into thinking that something that's true isn't true. Many things we pin on each other are just made-up lies the majority of the time. Your selection of words will either help or hinder someone from getting ahead. After all, your criticism should be geared toward improving the quality of life of individuals. Never use them for your personal issues.

Rule 7: *Never underestimate the power of your words. They can heal as well as hurt.*

EIGHT

MIND YOUR OWN BUSINESS

And why don't you do just that? Too many of us pretend to be solvers of problems that don't even concern us. Or another way of saying it is we cannot go around walking with a Superman or Wonder Woman label on our clothes. It's very easy to get into a world of trouble, but it's even more difficult to try and get out of a tight spot. In this respect, there is no one to blame but you. By not minding your own affairs, it tends to bring on needless arguments and conflicts that could be avoided. In addition, others will alienate themselves from you. So be honest and fair to you. Do you really know someone's situation by going around and sticking your nose in another person's business? Nine times out of ten, you don't. It's not a matter of who's right and who's wrong but a matter of keeping your feet firmly planted on the ground.

Why mind your affairs? Because you can avoid jealousy, envy, animosity, and enmity among your peers. One never knows what one is thinking or how one feels about someone else. And by doing so, we will never know the other party's situation as to what he's going through. Whether someone is right or wrong can be fifty-fifty. And this is a moot point. So always keep to your affairs because you'll never have the true answer. And you could be off base in your thinking. Many people are sensitive and secretive about their personal affairs. They don't want it broadcast all over the world because they'll never know who their friends and enemies are. By taking this approach, you can avoid a lot of loopholes that may haunt you. Don't be a busybody, going around spreading another's affair.

It is hard not to restrain yourself from becoming involved when two people are at war with each other. If you knew them, you would try to be a peacemaker by separating them. But on the other hand, if you saw two strangers who had a conflict without weighing in all the facts, then you would stay out of it. No one knows what might happen next. If you really cared about them, then let them work it out on their own terms. People do have their oddities and their moments. You're thinking one way, and someone else is thinking another way. Everyone has his or her own idea of dealing with unfortunate circumstances. There is a sea of different opinions in society.

One of the greatest coaches the game of professional football has ever produced goes by the name of Bill Parcells. Whatever team he coaches, he would tell his players to not get involved in personal decisions because it will affect the team's performance. If he decides to draft, sign free agents, or let someone go, that is his sole discretion. And if any player on his roster decided against it, he would levy them with fines.

In a courtroom setting, judges are dead set against anyone among the general public who calls out or are out of line while a session is going on. Of course, if anyone calls outs or gets out of line, the judge has the right to hold them in contempt of court and issue heavy fines, again at their sole discretion. And you wouldn't go around mulling if you saw cops apprehend criminals or suspects. The first thing a cop would tell you is, "Police business. Stay out." I know it's easier said than done because, if you witnessed a potential crime, you would want to lend a helping hand to spare someone's life. By all accounts, keep to your matters. This acronym sums up this closing paragraph-MYOB-mind your own business.

Rule 8: *Stop meddling in someone else's affairs.*

N I N E
DEALING WITH REJECTION

A young man was in the middle of the street outside of a nightclub, acting like a buffoon. He was just beside himself, making himself look silly in front of about thirty spectators, half of whom were women. He was shouting insults and other negative comments aimed at them for about five minutes. These unknown women stood around and gave him a hateful stare because of his derogatory remarks. It looked as though they were ready to beat him to a bloody pulp because he was putting them down in such a way that it became embarrassing for them. He told them that he didn't need them, that they were no good to him, and that he could do better without them. He even flung off his shirt, displayed his bare chest to them, and beat on it. He continued in such an inappropriate manner until, finally, his buddy came out and restrained him from further embarrassment. Those two exchanged their war of words, shouting at each other, until the disgruntled man decided to comport himself and return back to his rational behavior. Had he continued this unnecessary verbal assault on the innocent women, it might have ended traumatically for him that night. Eventually, he stopped and the insulted women and other curious spectators proceeded to their destinations. He went back inside. I don't know if the whole episode was due to the mere fact that his feelings were hurt or insulted. Moreover, it could have been that he was a masochist or he was overly intoxicated or he may have had a particular crush on a certain lady and she gave him the cold shoulder routine or he was just having an off night. One thing was emphatically clear about him. He took his personal rejections very seriously. He took it to the point where he could have spent a night in jail or in an emergency ward.

In one of television's top-rated shows, *American Idol,* a young lady contestant was auditioning for an once-in-a-lifetime opportunity to fly to Los Angeles and showcase her singing talents to the country and to the judges. She knew she could sing. She swore she was a gifted singer. And she knew she was going to tinsel town to be a qualified contestant and possibly sing her way to instant stardom. At least by her standards she thought so, but not by the judges' standards. They were unimpressed, voting her off the show. And as a result of this, she took the rejection personally. She did some unladylike things before the eyes of the nation, the other contestants, and the judges. In addition, she made some inappropriate remarks and did some other insulting body gestures aimed at them. One of the judges became offended and called for security to throw her out before things got worse. Such are the liabilities of rejection.

Free yourself from rejection. Whether we can accept it or not is another unfortunate ugly fact of life we have to cope with. Like in the preceding chapters on forgiveness, consistency, and criticism, we have to learn from it. We don't have to welcome it with open arms, but we must deal with it. By human nature, no one in God's colorful world takes being turned away very lightly. People want what they cannot have. But does that mean we have to appear clownish, act like an imbecile, or harm someone because we didn't get those things that we so deservedly desire? Not at all! We should never take a pessimistic view or look at the wrong side of being turned down. When one has ignored you for their personal intentions, it means that you should overlook them and proceed with your plans. No one can ever comprehend what one's dismissal of another means. It may very well be that they were not meant for each other in the first place. It may be political, they may have some side issues with you, or they just don't want to have anything to do with you. Just as everything is not for everybody, everybody is not for everybody as well. Because you can't always have what you want doesn't mean you should go around mulling in misery, commit some crazy act of suicide, and alienate those who love you dearly, or became annoyed and fed up at everybody and the world around you. I was taught in my childhood years that no matter whom you are, where you go, or what your status or rank in life is, you will receive a lifetime of rejection from those you come in contact with on a consistent basis. People are not in interested in your titles; they are interested in your testimonies.

Why do we have a difficult time being rejected by those we have a growing interest in? It could be that a higher source is telling us something for our own good. We are not going to get spoiled in all our doings at the expense of society. If we were to have our own way all the time, then we would become bored and would never know what it means to earn something worthwhile. Being tossed aside means you have to accept those things that are in your needs, not wanting those tangibles you can't have. Unless you were born into a wealthy family, your mission is to earn a paycheck so you can survive. Even the rich and famous receive their fair share of rejection. Being rejected means you learn to mature as a full-fledged citizen, appreciating those things that are a must for us, not those things that benefit us for our own pleasures. Think of your job situations. How many times have you had the door closed on you? Numerous times, I am quite sure. I can't think of any other place in the world where thousands of applicants get turned away, thanks to the decision of upper management. They may feel that certain candidates are not suitable for certain positions. Again, no one will ever know if politics is involved, if it's nepotism, or if the employer is interested in you or not. Speaking of becoming disinterested, a lot of factors are taken into consideration. Maybe your guise or how you present yourself is a major factor. The clothes you wear can tell the employer if you are right for the job. If you present yourself in a conservative fashion, then he may open the door for you. However, if you dress casually, then that could be a turnoff for him. Certain words that you say may either help or hinder you. Your words are who you are and what you live by. Some words may be too strong, some too weak, there may be too much verbosity or not enough. Few can really sell themselves to the employer. Lastly, some underhanded moves are likely to be pushed under the rug. Let's say the interviewer interviewed twenty applicants for that job. They were all good, but he had a specific candidate in mind. The other nineteen got neglected because that one person really impressed him. He stuck out to him like a sore thumb. You may be a prime candidate for a specific job. Since he has the authority, he has the last say. At any rate, these are just a few things to take into account as to why many get tossed aside.

Another area of concern is the dating game. Many relationships turn sour because both parties may have cheated on each other. I know that tons of people treat rejection like it's some kind of toxic material. Sometimes, this can lead to domestic violence and even death. Many boyfriend, girlfriend relationships and married couples take being turned away for whatever reason not so lightly. When people start acting irrationally, it could be due to the fact that they have been drinking too much alcoholic beverages or, perhaps, have turned to drugs to cope with his problems. Drinking can take away someone's rational ability to handle things in a way other people can understand. They could be mentally ill. And how you handle it is subjective. For example, four people can deal with it. One person may get themselves drunk. Another will say that he or she will go back the next night and feel he can do better the following day. Still yet, another person may feel that it's the end of his life. It is the same event, but people react differently to it. People need to look at it as if they are dealing with things in ways that are moving their lives forward or retrograding? Are they feeling better about themselves, trying to make a positive impact on the world? Or are they handling their life in a way that is self-destructive, self-defeating, or whatever? People can make choices around that. One may feel really depressed. He can choose to get help for that or stay in his house and live the life of a hermit. People can choose how they move on from being neglected. He may look back on his life and feel that, at that moment in time, his world was coming to an end. Now he may feel grateful that she didn't marry him or feel that that person wasn't the right choice. At any rate, one probably felt so monumental at that very moment.

Everything is situational. And it's how you deal with it. People have strong belief systems. And this is beneficial to them. If you believe in God, then there is a reason for why things happen the way it does. For instance, if something bad happens to you, you learn to grow from it and move on. Again, it depends on the person and their ability to recover. Sometimes, things happen that are superimposed. Let's say you grew up in a family where you got rejected a lot or got told you were a lousy person. When you become an adult and someone rejects you in a benign way, which cuts into a deep wound, then your reaction to that may not be on that event. It could be based on the fact that you have a history of rejection. That's tantamount to saying you're at the bottom of the barrel and someone still wants to pounce on you for their personal gratification.

It's always best to look at yourself objectively. Children get brainwashed. When you are little and someone tells you that you are no good and you mess up their life, then you are so vulnerable that you start to believe those things that are not objective. That's the person or parent, who is in power, acting out on their self-inflicting wounds. And the reason why they do that is because their parents probably told them they were no good. If one were to approach you with that mind-set, then help them see themselves in a positive way. If one was to act out negatively to you, then that has nothing to do with you. That is that person's problem, not yours. Consider this food for thought: if someone were to insult you to your face, saying stuff like, "You are stupid", and "You can't do it" would you feed off their negative comments or just completely ignore them? I would hope you would do the latter. What one would say to another in a degrading fashion means their words have no value or merit.

Don't kid yourself into thinking that the world is about to come to an abrupt end because you've been rejected. Here's something to think about. You have rejected others as well, due to your circumstances. There may have very well been someone whom you wanted to avoid at all costs. You realized that they were not the right person(s) for you. In order not to carry the burden of this matter any further, you had to turn them loose at some juncture in your life. They, perhaps, felt neglected and downcast, asking themselves, "What's wrong with me?" or "What did I do to deserve that kind of treatment?" At any rate, they had to pick their lives up and start all over again. Like I mentioned earlier about job situations, you may have rejected an offer from an employer as well. You felt the job does not meet your financial requirements, the hours are not flexible enough to suit your taste, or the job was such a turnoff that you had to let it go. Lastly, you sent a stern message to a person because he created such a hostile environment. His personality was so obnoxious that it came to a point where you had to tell him to go away and not make matters any worse. Like criticism and respect, rejection is a two-way revolving door.

Rejection, to so many, is a bitter pill to swallow. Don't take it to the point where you'll hold it against someone, until your last living days are upon you. In the meantime, turn all of your personality forces, energies, and attention to that one person who is for you, not against you. Life is way too short to worry about one who neglects you for their own reasons. They may realize one day that the move they made was an egregious mistake letting you go for someone else who wasn't worth anything to them in the first place. Don't take your rejection to the fourth degree or beyond that, become annoyed at everybody whom you come in contact with, or commit some foolish act of suicide. You have to look at rejection with open-mindedness and fairness. This is not the best remedy for being neglected. Like in the preceding paragraphs, concerning jobs, if an employer closes the door in your face, then look to the door that has been opened for you. If someone shuts you off from his world, look to the one that is opening new avenues before your eyes. Someday, you may look back and be thankful. Whether it's personal or not, keep going. You have many obstacles to hurdle over. And unfortunately, rejection is one of them

Rule 9: *Sometimes, not getting what we want is a blessing in disguise.*

TEN

VIOLENCE NO MORE

A young boy, looking like he was around seven or eight, walks into a barbershop with his father, waiting for his turn to have a haircut. I was mulling around with others, when, to my surprise, for no apparent reason at all, the child approaches me and says, "Do you want to box me?" I stood there, gazing at him. I couldn't believe such words would come out of his mouth. "No! I don't want to box you," was my reply. "Fighting has never resolved anything and it never will." That was something to think about! He didn't know me. I didn't know if he was a child so bold to approach a stranger in that fashion, had that mind-set instilled in him, perhaps from his father, or may have been joking. Either way, he's going to grow up with that mentality in him. I didn't want to rush to judgment so quickly. I presumed that his father may have gotten into some melee, in his heydays. I assume that every time he gets into a senseless altercation or a heated argument with someone, his first words will be, "Do you want to fight me?" Such is our lot as full-fledged adult citizens. There have been many times when we let our emotions, frustrations, angers, and resentments run away with us. The first thing we would resort to, in all likelihood, is some form of domestic violence.

Violence should be the first thing at the top of your hate list to eradicate, just like how God hates sin and it's at the top of his hate list. Many of us welcome this conundrum with open arms, fall prey to it, and use it as a basis to get the crux of our customary arguments across to others. But it always backfires in the long run. Too many people have fallen victim to this age-old common denominator. Does it pay to use it? No! You pay a heavy fine, like alienating those you socialize with, getting in trouble with the law, and, sometimes, signing your own death certificate, if you know what I mean. Never resort to any kind of physical behavior to make a valid point or make you feel justified. All violence is an insane waste of energy.

There are many factors to consider that lead to all types of onslaught. Some of them are arguing constantly, cheating on your partner or your spouse, money, jealousy, and, sometimes, sudden termination from the workforce. Nowadays, we argue about things that are irrelevant or meaningless. Family members argue daily. It could be that some feel threatened by the fact that some siblings have more going for them, enabling them to go further in life. Jealousy overtakes them. We have child abuse, elder abuse, and some intimate partners being abused. Some cannot control their emotions. In the dating game, we become so entangled with the other party that we find it impossible to let go. We may feel that, at some juncture, we may lose them to another person. The police reports that most crimes occur within homes. By the time the cops get there, the person is already deceased. This could be another factor that leads to out-of-control anger. Moreover, plenty believe in dishonesty. If they feel they can get away with such foolishness, they will try it. Some will try cheating if they can. Depending on the individual, some will walk away from you. Yet, others will prefer an altercation before finally turning you lose. Lastly, when it comes to employment, some workers have taken being terminated to the fifth degree.

Many times, it has turned sour when employers dismiss workers. It could be that some workers weren't suitable for certain positions or something personal may have been brewing for quite some time between an employer and his employee. As a result of all of this, the situation grew nasty and ugly in their relationship. These are just a few ingredients that can lead to senseless violence.

I want you to visualize that you are traveling in a time machine, reliving four separate incidents that are prime examples of physical brutality. Two are local and two are national. Depending on you, as the reader, I don't know if you can recount all four events. But I do know that two of them made national headlines. Starting in chronological order, we have two nightclub acts and two riotous acts that triggered off this entire melee. First we begin with a discotheque incident.

December 30, 1984

New Year's Eve is supposed to be a time when old, tired, and dreary thoughts are cast away and new ideas and visions come alive. It's a hybrid of wild celebrations, prolonged partying, singing, lively dancing, good eating, and praying. It's supposed to be a time when you let your imagination run free with you. It appeared at a popular Philadelphia nightspot called The Library Discotheque. The disc jockey was happily spinning songs of delight for the audience. Everyone was either mulling around, conversing with one who struck his or her interest, dancing, drinking, observing, or just in a relaxed mode. All were eagerly waiting for the arrival of a brand new year. It was going to be a morning of fun and laughs. Or at least the raucous crowd thought so. As things turned out, it didn't happen that way. Everyone was in for a rude surprise.

Three unknown persons caused a commotion to happen. Apparently, they got into a scuffle with management over something that was petty. One will never know if they were out looking for trouble, misunderstanding, or whatever. As a result of this, they were asked to leave. They stubbornly refused to. Management called the bouncers to escort them away. And again, they didn't comply. By not leaving, they got into a fight with the bouncers. Punches were exchanged. Beer cans and bottles, drinking glasses, or what have you were thrown every, which way, but more so in the directions of the bouncers. People started scurrying to the nearest exits as quickly as possible, fearing what might happen next. Even the disc jockey stopped playing the records, believing his life might be in jeopardy. Had it not been for an off-duty cop, this senseless brawl could have gotten worse. But it didn't. The policeman had to shoot two of them to bring things under control and quell down the nervous crowd. The third suspect managed to get away intact. About thirty cop cars surrounded the entire area, making sure no one was seriously injured or even killed for that matter. Still, people were either scampering for their cars or disappearing quickly into the pitch night, running as fast and as far as possible from danger. Fortunately, no one else was seriously hurt or injured. The two men were apprehended and taken into police custody after being treated for their gunshot wounds. This popular nightclub had to shut its doors down because the neighbors and community leaders didn't want to see this kind of drama unfold on their side of the town. Let's give credit where credit is due. Had it not been for the officer, it may have been a night of triumph for some and may have very well been a morning of tragedy for others. But it wasn't.

September 4, 1989

Labor Day weekend is supposed to be a time when all outdoor festivities of the summer are about to come to an end. It's a time when outdoor picnics, beach parties, camping, hiking, or other interests are ready for hibernation. So it was for Virginia Beach, presumably the largest beach resort in the world. It's more or less a quiet beach city with very little shows and activities happening to upset the apple cart. Maybe it is but not on this particular weekend. A lot of drama unfolded here, drawing attention to a national maelstrom.

This popular beach city experienced one of its worst disasters in its history. Thousands of college students, from across the country, gather here for their annual Greek fest activities. In addition, other young people came here to see the fraternities and sororities participate in their exciting step. In addition, other young people came here to see the fraternities and sororities in this exciting event. However, many became intoxicated and rioted in the streets, breaking windows, looting clothing stores and small shops, and vandalizing property. The black college students reasoned that racism was the main concern, which lead to their belligerent attitudes. Many students said that the cops were out of line by attacking everyone who was black or a looter. And to protest their disapproval of the police brutality, many wore T-shirts with two slogans that read: "It's a black thing you wouldn't understand" and "It's a cop thing; we'll make you understand." The mayor had to call the army, the National Guard, and military police and beef up more security to protect the innocent and quell down the irate rioters and protesters. The incident spread throughout the country as millions witnessed the fracas.

In the aftermath of the riots, community leaders and activists convened as to what triggered it and sought for a remedy to see that this incident would never happen again. Even the local NAACP branch headquartered there, sought preventative measures such as teaching cops better arresting techniques. Local authorities replayed video tapes of the police brutality imposed on students who were disorderly and were destroying store owners' property. To this very day, no one knows for sure what ignited the 1989 riots. There is widespread speculation that racism was the main cause. Since then, a special task force was established to prevent this turmoil from ever happening again. Like a careless driver putting a dent on your car, the riots left a dent on the city's image.

April 29, 1992

In March of 1991, a motorist, Rodney King, was stopped by the Los Angeles police for driving up to 115 mph. He resisted arrest and fought with four cops, who managed to beat him mercilessly, fifty-six times with nightsticks. His bones were broken in eleven places. An amateur photographer, George Holiday, videotaped the infamous beating. It was played and replayed numerous times across the country and around the world. The grand jury deliberated on King's beating and came to a sound conclusion that the cops were innocent. In the final analysis, the jury's decision to acquit the cops, the black community, citizens, and viewers became disgruntle and angry. This was the "flicker that spread into a flame."

In South Central Los Angeles, riots broke out. These would become the worst riots on American soil. They resulted in arsons, looting, and even murder. Small shops and businesses were destroyed. Fires were set, thousands of injuries occurred, commercial buildings were destroyed, and many people lost their lives. On live television, an innocent truck driver, Reginald Denny, was pulled from his truck by four gang members, and beaten unconscious, with his skull being crushed by a stone. The attackers then danced around his battered body, celebrating their infamous victory. But it was temporary because a fellow truck driver, watching on his television from his nearby house managed to come to his aid and save him from death. The four suspects were later captured and arrested on criminal charges.

These riots are like a disease spreading rapidly to other parts of the body because other cities had similar incidents like the Los Angeles riots. For example, in Philadelphia, on the University of Pennsylvania campus, students became livid and started protesting the jury's decision to overlook the cops' actions. They were demonstrating, marching around the campus chanting in their anger, "No justice, no peace!" The mayor of Philadelphia, Ed Rendell, came on live television for about twenty minutes and delivered his speech, urging everyone to remain calm and rational in the wake of the Rodney King ordeal. He was speculating that similar incidents might have unfolded here. As a result of this nightmarish act, King and other civil rights activists and leaders, reappeared a couple of days later, trying to quell the irate rioters and bring the ethnic communities back into harmony. What he said must have resounded in everyone's ears that day. He said, "Now can we all get along?" It must have been the right medicine for them, because shortly thereafter, order was restored and everything was normal.

March 27, 1995

There is a popular strip joint up in the hills of Reading, Pennsylvania, called Al's Diamond Cabaret. On this balmy night, three hundred guests came out to have a good time and see a world-renowned entertainer, La Toya Jackson, do a striptease for them. They were yelling at the top of their lungs for her to take her clothes off. What they got was a tease all right! La Toya didn't take it off at all. The rowdy crowd became distraught, asking for management to refund their money. She left the stage, leaving her audience angry as beer cans, bottles, and fists started flying. Things quieted down quickly. But the crowd remained angry. Backstage, they asked her why she didn't take her clothes off for them. She said, "I don't lower my standards for anyone." For her fans, it was a night of teasing, not fun and laughs.

I gave you four separate incidents on a minor and a major scale. It ranged from two local nightclub acts to two national racial riots. Hopefully, we can all learn from our unique experiences. We should never travel these paths to justify our course of actions. It may be easier said than done for many. Sometimes, it's the right thing to do to avoid a senseless conflict. Certainly, violence is not the road to take. I have written an oath to stop any kind of domestic violence that you may feel you are uncomfortable with. It is one that should be written on your memory for the rest of your lives. It is one that should be at the top of your priority list for establishing a healthy and harmonious relationship among your peers. You should pass it on to those in need of reforming themselves. It reads:

Let it be written, let it be said, let it be known that, henceforth, I do solemnly swear that, never again in life, in any way, shape, or form, on any matter, shall I engage in an act of domestic violence, that I may feel is redeemable to further justify my cause, just to prove my points valid to others, so help me God.

At what does it pay to use any kind of fury? It costs you plenty. You alienate those around you. By creating a hostile environment, people tend to avoid you, fearing that some altercation might break out over nothing. To lose your sanity and become livid at the hands of another moron, friends, family, and acquaintances distance themselves from you. You lose your self-worth, self-esteem, rational behavior, believing that the only solution to mastering a problem is through some type of physical abuse. It does cost you a great deal, especially in the long run. To act like some ravaging beast says a lot of you. The majority of your life, you walk a lonely road, especially when you're trying to win someone over to your side of the story. And it is a *faux pas*. Sometimes, to put an end to utter nonsense, one may need some professional intervention, like anger management. Those who crave for drama all of the time are miserable to be around with. They may have a deeply embedded grudge against society and the world at large.

In these next two riveting examples, I give you an account of two ordinary people, who turned out to be unsung heroes. They had to employ some means of violence to save other's lives, not take it away. One fought literally; the other fought figuratively. One was an entity. The other one was a nonentity. Both did heroic acts to counteract their enemies' plan.

The great abolitionist, Frederick Douglass, spent all of his life fighting for justice and equal rights to free blacks and slaves. On this special occasion, he had to engage in a physical fight to save his life and others. Experiencing life as a free man, he and his associates were speaking in the state of Indiana against slavery. And to be more specific, it took place in the woods. After constructing a platform to speak on, about sixty of the roughest looking men, called the mob, approached them from out of nowhere. They had come, not to parley, but to fight. They ordered Frederick and his companions to "be silent" or their lives would be in jeopardy. Douglass and others tried to dissuade them, but to no avail. The mob tore down the platform, severely attacked one of his friends, knocking out several of his teeth, and then dealt a heavy blow on the back of his head, cutting his scalp, and knocking him to the ground. Douglass saw this and joined the melee with a stick, trying to rescue his friend. This attracted other mob members toward him, of whom three beat him savagely, knocking him to the ground and knocking him unconscious. The mob quickly mounted their horses and drove off. When he came around, he was treated for his wounds, but found out that his right hand was broken. It healed but not completely. Douglass never regained full use of his hands, afterward[1]. Clearly, this was a setup to derail him.

In another time, an Irishman, Thomas Hickey, one of Washington's bodyguards, was persuaded to join the Tory conspiracy. He took a black mistress, Phoebe Fraunces, to be his housekeeper.

Hickey had decided to poison Washington, with plans to have Phoebe put the poison in her boss's favorite dish—green peas. Pretending not to go along with the plans until she had further details, the young, black woman encouraged her lover to give her more and more information.

The evening came when Washington was to die. Hickey gave the poison to Phoebe and watched her mixed it into the green peas. He stood silently while the dish was served. Suddenly, astonishment crossed Hickey's face. Washington threw the peas out the window and watched as the chickens greedily pecked at them and then fell over and died. Arrested and tried by court martial, Hickey was sentenced to death by hanging. Twenty

---

[1] Douglass, Life and Times of Frederick Douglass, 234.

thousand onlookers witnessed the first military execution in the nation's history.[2]

Thus, history records that it was a black woman who helped prevent the assassination of George Washington, by gathering enough evidence. Had it not been for this ever-alert woman, Washington, not Lincoln, would have been America's first ever president to be killed in office. And this would have altered the course of history a great deal.

Philadelphia far surpassed other major American cities in unenviable ugly statistics. It had the highest homicide rate in the years of 2005 and 2006. In both years, the numbers were slightly over the four-hundred mark. All of these violent crimes can be attributed to gun violence, gang members, drug dealers, organized crime, and, basically, people who lack education, people who have no goals, aims, or values. What's even more alarming is that these crimes were committed by people between the ages of eighteen to twenty-five years old. These young lions have a lot of pride and dignity, but it's headed in the wrong direction. Most of these senseless crimes occurred within an urban setting. For example, a young person who doesn't know the true meaning of life takes it for granted. From his microcosm, he doesn't know how life truly operates or what it has in store for him. He hasn't been out in the real world long enough to appreciate the good things that life can provide. Being young, naive, aggressive, and somewhat apathetic, he views his world as that of the old, rugged "Wild West", where the only way to clean up any bad or unacceptable activities taking place on the streets is to kill at random. Such is his perspective. But such an act is erroneous and antiquated nowadays. These thugs, hoodlums, robbers, or whoever that go around different playgrounds, schoolyards, small stores and shops, killing at will for no apparent reason, are deemed monsters or animals. In due time,

---

[2] "Let History Record That a Black Woman Prevented the Assassination of George Washington, the Father of Our Country," 20.

they do get their just rewards down the road. That's equivalent to saying you cheat on an exam. You may get away sometimes, but sooner or later, you slip up and get caught, paying a severe penalty. As with these inconsiderate bullies and brutes, they eventually become a victim of their own circumstances. Moreover, these ridiculous crimes have put a hamper on Philadelphia's businesses and population to a large extent. Thousands of tourists who would love to take a bird's-eye's view of this township won't do so, fearing their lives might be taken from them over something thought to be trivial and inane. Some businesses have folded up and relocated to another section of the country. Likewise, these citizens are doing the same. The city's population is on the decline.

It is morally wrong to kill just for the sake of killing. Something has to be done to put an abrupt end to this bellicose nature. Like in the Rodney King situation, we are letting the wrong people take control of our streets and neighborhoods and doing absolutely nothing about it. Too many citizens appear indifferent, carefree, and unconcerned to the needs of others. It is about high time that we put a stoppage to these senseless crimes and take back our community and streets. Politicians, community rights activists, lawmakers, church leaders, concerned citizens, and some celebrities have all convened, held rallies, protests, meetings, and some fund-raising events to do away with these miscreants and their wrongdoings. They have championed to make Philadelphia's streets safe and the town a productive one. America's fifth largest metropolis still has some in-house cleaning to do to right its wrongs. But in the meantime, these violent criminals have already tarnished the city's image to a degree. And rightly so, they should be put away forever and forgotten about. Philadelphia, once thought of as the "city of brotherly love," has now become the "city of brotherly loathe."

On another occasion, on the hot, sweltering streets of Philadelphia, in the summer of 2000, he was running from the cops for eleven days, committing crimes he shouldn't have committed. Some of his crimes were carjacking a woman's car, carrying out ten robberies and four assaults, driving on sidewalks, heading the wrong way down a one-way street, blowing through stop signs, racing down a closed street for playing children, and buzzing past mourners leaving a funeral. Moreover, he was under the influence of drugs. He gave way to two infamous chases by the police. In the first chase, ten officers fired a series of forty-six shots at him in a crowded neighborhood. The second one ended with him being pulled from a car and being pummeled by officers. He got into a scuffle with some of these cops before he was subdued and taken into police custody. His name is Thomas Jones.

His infamous beating, like Rodney King's, was shown across the country and around some parts of the world by a news helicopter. A grand jury examined his beatings and came to the conclusion that the fourteen cops involved in the fracas committed no crimes. They were exonerated. This shocked the nation and the world. It drew outrage and anger from black and civic leaders of the city. In a 190-page report by the grand jury, they found numerous things on Thomas Jones. On that particular day, because of his actions, he had it coming. The president of the NAACP branch in Philadelphia, Jerry Mondesire, was upset at the jury's decision. He felt that their decision would denigrate the city's image and its history. He and other community leaders felt that their findings were wrong and inconclusive. Aside from these facts, this unknown assailant had some bad genes in him. Eventually, it landed him in jail a long time.

In one of the previous chapters, I wrote about celebrity crucifixion. This time, it's not with words but with fists. I'm talking about two titans of the hip-hop music industry. They are Chris Brown and Rihanna. What we have here is two conflicting stories of interests. One February night, both were to show up at the prestigious Grammy awards show. Rihanna was to perform for the national audience. It wasn't meant to be. Neither one got there because they had a silly lover's spat over nothing. It escalated in to domestic violence. No one will ever know what caused it, except for those two. As a result of this, both got into a physical altercation due to sex. According to the news media, it was learned that she passed on a sexually transmitted disease to him, which she knew about. Chris went hysteric over this matter. While they were on their way to the show, she informed him, causing him to go ballistic on her. He gave her a black eye, a swollen lip, and some more nicks and bruises on her face. She, in return, started punching him like crazy, trying to defend herself from more physical torture. Moreover, he threatened to kill her, when she got to his place. Rihanna got out of his car and tracked down the police, who, in turn, arrested him on the spot. The next day, her battered face was front-page material on virtually every newspaper in America. Both of them have a wide fan base. But the public became outraged and incensed at Chris, more so than at her, because he was a man and women are considered the weaker sex between the two genders. The national media got a hold of this story and took it to the fourth degree. Another way of putting it is this story got blown out of proportion. Chris felt the public's venom for brutally attacking Rihanna over their minor differences. Many people called in on every television and radio station and voiced their opinions about women falling prey to domestic violence and how to recover from it. Even people on television talk shows became livid over what had transpired. Community groups and activists wanted to get involved over what had transpired. Many vented their anger at him, wanting to keep Chris in jail for a long time, saying he didn't have to use such tactics to prove his point. Some even wanted her to break off their relationship, suggesting she should move on in another direction with her life.

 Her version of her story was while she was at his place preparing for the show, they got into a shouting match. Angry words and threats were exchanged. He became frustrated, lunging at her, threatening he was going to kill her if she left. That's when she called the cops to have him arrested for going out of control.

On the other hand, Chris had his fair share of defenders defending his cause. Many claimed she drove him to doing such an atrocious act by keeping the secret to herself. Many say she should have forewarned him before having sexual intercourse. His cousin had a different account of the story. He claims that Chris was defending himself, because women like to fight as well as men. Chris, eventually, apologized for his wrongdoings. Later on, it was learned that Rihanna wanted to get back with him, saying she still loves him. Many argued that if she wanted to be him, then why did she have him arrested? One is falsely accusing the other of lying. One story contradicts the other. No one will ever know who threw the first stone or who the perpetrator was. Depending on how you view it, both of them were right and wrong for such irrational behavior. And years from now, this saga will die down to the point where no one really cares.

Never use violence as a mechanism to prove your point to others. It won't do you any good. And it will never prove anything over the long haul. When you create a hostile environment around those you deal with, you're digging a hole for yourself. It is a known fact that violence begets violence, crime breeds crime, and man will, ultimately, try to destroy man in such a way that it can turn into a major issue. Since the beginning of time, violence is still a liability we have to tackle and address, unfortunately. It is sad to say there will never be an end to this age- old dilemma because it is a common denominator, which has been passed down from ages to ages. We should be more concerned and caring citizens than ever before. We should never let the bad take complete control of the streets, stores, and our neighborhoods. Our children and our senior citizens should never have to bow down to this faulty approach. It is fifty-fifty in that many welcome this dilemma, instead of opposing it. Those who favor it, prefer a mass destruction, a primitive approach—sticks, knives, stones, revolvers, or whatever—to prove their points. Sometimes this method could backfire and land you in three places: a hospital bed, a jail cell, or a cemetery. But those who oppose such brutal behavior would prefer a more rationalized, civilized method: protocol, tactfulness, and diplomacy. We're all going to pass on to another life one day. We don't have to rush our times on earth, at the hands of thugs, hoodlums, gangsters, drugs, drunkenness, suicide, and yes, the unavoidable domestic violence. Perhaps, they invest in that. It doesn't mean you have to go along with their programs to justify your point. Using any form of physical abuse will prove nothing at the end of the day. It never has and never will. There is a saying which says *you have to stop and smell the roses along the way.* By employing this tactic, you can prolong your life and reap the joys and pleasures associated with it. I do hope you will emphasize the latter and deemphasize the former in sustaining a conciliatory relationship among your peers. Whatever it costs, do away with any form of fury. And yes! I couldn't agree anymore with what Rodney King once said, "Now, can we all get along?" Now, can we?

Rule 10: *Those who live by the sword die by the sword.*

ELEVEN
A GOOD THING FROM A BAD SITUATION

Have you ever been in one of those situational experiences where it seems like there is no way out? I'm sure you have plenty of times. It's like walking inside a dark tunnel with no light at the end. Suddenly, you see some daylight, letting you know that there is an opening at the very end. In nearly every aspect of our lives, we have encountered some unexplained circumstance that didn't sit well with us. And it could have ranged from failed marriages, job layoffs, unfair housing, inferior schooling, or even something that was leisurely. Whatever, it can be a learning process in which to grow and move on from. They are in the same manner as finding the right job that suits our needs. For instance, whenever we finish in some institution of higher learning, many of us have to take some tedious monotonous job just to put food on our tables. We cannot always get what we want at first. We have to put up with a lot just to reach our ultimate goal. Likewise, our health issues are a primary concern nowadays. At an early age, we don't value life as much or take things like heart attacks as seriously. When we are in our twenties or thirties, we tend to be lighthearted and take what comes our way in stride. A good example is, when we walk the streets at night, there are seen and unseen dangers. When we use the streets, amid the uncanny dangerous activities that occur, we feel that no harm or danger will come our way. We come off with an air of invincibility, thinking that we are in complete control of our destinations and this world. But then, something unexpected always happens to us to bring us back down-to- earth. We are dealt a reality check to bring us back in harmony with our surroundings. And I am quite sure this is one of those unforeseen situational experiences that take hold of us.

On the other side of the coin, our unique circumstances are as different as the colors in a color spectrum. Like in any social club setting, all of our personalities are different from the person standing next to you. Again, let us take the case of health issues. We all contact some disease at some juncture of our lives. Some are treatable. And some are life threatening. Until some miracle medicine is invented, we have to endure the repercussions of these detrimental diseases. Some people recover quickly, enabling them to go about their daily chores as planned. Some may take awhile to recuperate. Others have reached the end of their life's journeys, hopefully passing on to a better life. Take the case of a school environment. In a classroom setting, there is always a faster learner and a slow learner. Some people are ahead of their times in learning. Some have to labor hard before putting the finishing touches on a project. And some never can grasp the concept of what you're talking about. They may need some assistance or tutoring to boost their morale. Clearly, we have no control over things to come because sometimes such occurrences are "acts of God" which nobody can solve. In short, these are some of the ingredients, either tangibles or intangibles, which relate to our sound situational experiences. Like your opinions, your statuses can be good, bad, or indifferent, depending on how you view it. In a finer sense, this is your open-book to read.

Speaking of one that was intangible, I was involved in a touch-and-go one. It was a bad, unfortunate one to learn from. But it was my learning tree to grow from. It was like I had no control over what was to come. Mine was, no more or less, different than the next person standing alongside of me. Within a thirteen-month span, I had no idea of what was to transpire. I was having one mishap after another. There were times I kept asking myself, "Why me? What did I do to deserve this harsh treatment?" I don't know if the gods upstairs were trying to send me some signal or trying to convey a message to me about something. At any rate, these traumatic experiences were unavoidable, uncontrollable, trying, and telling. Was I doing something wrong to disturb them? Or was my life headed in the wrong direction? Still to this very day, I cannot figure out why such ill-fated occurrences unfolded right before my eyes. As I start this saga, you will be surprised at some of the mishaps that were at the center of these learning lessons. It wasn't my health. It wasn't my job. It wasn't my intimate relationship. It was my car that was the center of attention. That's right! My car! It was the focal point of these disturbances. There were some other minor incidents involved, but for the most part, my car was my major concern. And this is how it all began:

Spring 1991

Cars are one of those expensive, precious commodities that not everyone can afford. Those who own one are to handle it with extreme care. I've made up in my mind that, for the remainder of my life, I would never go without one. Many times in life, we have no idea what the future holds in store for us. That includes a series of unfortunate events that happened to my auto and me. As for me, I don't know if I was slightly getting ahead of my time, becoming meticulous in my routines, or it was just one of those mishaps that happen to us. All of these happenings began on a balmy spring day. The temperature was normal. The weather was ideal. The day was picture-perfect clear. But the occurrences weren't.

I was only three blocks from my final destination when I was involved in a nasty crash. It wasn't my fault because I was in a complete standstill when the accident unfolded. The impact of the crash was so shocking and great that it felt like lightning struck me.

Luckily for me, I had a proper headrest installed because if I didn't, I might have sustained further head and neck injuries. The driver, who rear-ended me, forced my car to rear- end another one in front of me. There I was, right in the middle of a three-car collision. Luckily for me, I was fortunate enough to get out and walk around without receiving any serious injuries. The driver appeared to be in his late teens to early twenties. He had the nerve to ask me why I suddenly stopped before him. I told him that the light had turned red and there were others cars before me. What was I to do? Run over them? As I proceeded to get some information from him, he drove off in a hurried pace. By the time the cops got there, he was out of sight and out of harm's way. I never saw him again. Clearly, this was a case of a hit-and-run accident.

Man was I ever livid and upset about this misadventure. If I had gotten my hands on him, I would have strangled every ounce of life out of his system. But then again, I had to remind myself to remain calm and rational because anger and retaliation never accomplishes anything. Lots of times, these young thugs may have some form of weapon on them. Their motto is to *hit first and ask questions later*. I was careful not to pass judgment on him too quickly. You never know what he might have done. And you never know what these young lions are on. He could have been on drugs, intoxicated with liquor, stole that vehicle or what. He got away scot-free, leaving me standing there with a wrecked car and sore neck. Both the front and rear ends looked like a tractor trailer plowed into it. He left my car and my day in ruins.

Summer 1991

I had just returned from the seashore with my sisters in the wee hours of the morning. Tired, worn out, and sleepy from the long day's activities and travel, I was ready to call it quits. A good night's sleep was my remedy. And the place I resided in was an ideal one. It was a quiet community with very little activities happening.

When I dozed off, I presumed that everything would be normal when the next day came. And to be more specific, I was convinced that my parking lot was a safe haven, safe and secure from any wrongdoings like the ones that take place out in the streets. Or was it? The reason I say so is because never has my car been tampered or broken in to, until I woke up the next day. When I did, I was in for another rude awakening.

Apparently, some hoodlums broke into my car. They wrecked my steering column, broke the passenger window on the driver's side, and stole my car radio. It was obvious that they were looking for drugs, money, or some other valuables I may have left in the car. "Not again!" I thought to myself, "This can't be happening to me. Why me? Why pick on my car?" I was angry and frustrated. My car is my main mode of transportation. Why was this bad karma suddenly happening to my car and me? What did I do to deserve this harsh treatment? My plans to get on with my tasks were once again derailed, like it was three months earlier. I reasoned that things happen for a reason that we have no answers for, until later on.

My affairs had gone, not from bad to worse, but from worse to treacherous. After all the damages and repairs were estimated and completed, I got my car back. Again, these miscreants got away clean like that aggressive driver did months earlier. And again, coming home from work, I had another minor mishap. This time it was not my car but on my job. I broke my thumb. It happened in the last hour on the job. To try to drive home in pain is no good feeling. The doctor diagnosed it as a hairline fracture. That forced me out of work for quite some time. There I was again, sitting at home and agonizing over my car and my thumb. It was a very tedious way of living. I felt like a prisoner in my house. Moreover, I had to put my other activities on the shelf, until my thumb completely healed. A fractured bone on any part of your body will take it's time to heal. Such an injury won't heal overnight. There I was, sitting at home, musing to myself about the ill-fate of my car and thumb. Such was my ill-luck.

Fall 1991

My car had been repaired. My thumb had completely healed. And the weather was beginning to break for the fall season. Nothing could be more ideal and finer than to see that everything was back to normal. At least, it appeared to be. I was going about my daily chores as usual. As I was getting into my car, I noticed that another ill-fated incident transpired. Somebody busted my rear window, or at least, it appeared that way, until I had all of the details in place. For the first time in my life, I had a growing concern and feared that someone was out to get me. And I didn't rule out the possibility of foul play. You'll never know who is watching you. Yet, you can't go around in a state of paranoia over every minor incident. But I was becoming more suspicious than ever before as to why these mishaps kept on happening to me and to my auto. People are envious of the smallest things you possess. If you have something that somebody else wants but don't have, then that makes them more jealous of you and your belongings. I filed a report with the police, but that didn't do any good. When you need the cops, they are nowhere. When you don't need them, they are everywhere. Nonetheless, the cops came and wrote up a report over what had transpired. It was evening when this occurrence took place. I rushed home to inform my parents of what happened this time. Even they had their growing concerns and fears over what might happen next. (What else could happen to this poor old, picked-on car? Was somebody out to steal it for their own use? Or should I trade it in for a newer model?) Maybe the forces were telling me that my life was headed in the wrong direction. But I was doing no wrong as far as I could see. I mused it was time for me to sit down, analyze it, and regroup what I was doing. As far as I could see, I wasn't doing anything out of the ordinary to bring on these troubles. But these bad happenstances didn't see it that way.

The next morning, as I was leaving to take it to a repair shop, I happened to glance on the backseat while getting my belongings.

To my dismay, I noticed a small object lying on the floor. Surprise overtook me. To think that someone may have been bothering with my vehicle was now a non-issue. It was a stone. Someone had inadvertently thrown it in the wrong direction, not seeing where my auto was parked. A day earlier, I noticed that some mischievous kids were horsing around with each other across the railroad tracks. I didn't play that much attention to what they were doing. Children will be children for ours' sake! Suddenly, I had solved my own mystery. Nobody was out to carjack me, as I had presumed. It was one of those unavoidable things that needed no logical explanation. I should have known better. When I was a child, we did mischievous things like rock throwing. I use to do all sorts of bad things that got me in hot water with my parents. Since I've matured, I've outgrown those negative feelings. At any rate, my growing suspicion of somebody after me was relieved at once. The heaviness that took its toll on me for about six months was gone in a twinkle of an eyelash. Thank God this incident was on a minor scale, not on a major one. It was all right to drive and I was safe. And my well- being was safe for the moment.

Summer 1992

Another winter had passed by with no more minor or major disturbances. And I am happy to report that this is the final episode of my car saga. It was another time, another season, but unfortunately, there were new hapless events. In the summer months, we get those severe, unanticipated violent thunderstorms. The strong winds that accompany them are pretty violent themselves. Wind can be very destructive. It can tear down parts of houses, knock over wired telephone poles, and uproot trees. That is exactly what happened to this poor old, beat-up, renovated car. It was one of those unexpected thunderstorms that can last for up to an hour or so. When it passed through my area, the telephone poles were blown away, severe flooding had occurred, and the trees were uprooted. Some were partially knocked down. For the umpteenth time, my car had been victimized. I glanced outside my door to see if everything was all right. It wasn't. The severity of the storm had caused part of the tree to drop a huge tree branch on the top of my car roof. What else could go wrong this time? (Like I've said earlier, have you ever been in a situation where you felt like you were at the bottom of the barrel? I have. That's what it felt like at that moment. I mused, "Is this déjà vu?" It was almost a year ago that these terrible experiences happened. The reason I state this is because three weeks earlier I had lost my mother, due to death. I was still sad and reeling from her sudden departure from life.) Now, my car was my major issue once more. The tree trunk hit the roof with such an impact that it left a huge dent on it. It was like a large rock from out of nowhere hit it. For the fourth time in nearly a year, I was handicapped.

Why were all of these bad experiences happening to me? What does it mean? Was I doing something wrong that some higher source was trying to send me a message? What was going to happen next? I had asked myself a dozen of these thought-provoking questions, trying to theorize these unexplained events. Frustrated, confused, and somewhat downcast, I was looking for answers from within. Finally, it dawned on me that I might have to readjust my life to a degree. Perhaps, it was going in the wrong direction, moving slightly too fast, or it was just one of those plain unfortunate things that happens to all of us from time to time. I've concluded that we have to endure some difficulties to reach our destinations. Everybody, at some juncture in their lives, has had some rocky paths to travel. We have no control over unseen situations that life brings to the table. We have to weather the storm, learn from it, and help another who may be in the same boat we're in. Today, I look back and thank my lucky stars that it was a learning process. I've learned to master the good from any bad situations that come my way.

A Successful Formula

What good could conceivably come out of any bad or trying situation? Many, I am quite sure. And there are many factors to consider. No good ever came out of my car ordeal. It was just one of those unexplainable, unavoidable, unfortunate happenings. All I could do was learn from these mishaps. Some can be helped and some cannot. First, whatever events you're dealing with, it is for a reason. It is to make and mold you into a strong individual. It may be preparing you for challenging things that lie ahead. This is a rough world in which we reside. And we have many loopholes to overstep. Every day that passes, we become older and wiser to the things that surround us. And we learn something new every day. If one of life's challenging forces were to meet you head-on and unexpectedly, then you would know better how to respond to its liabilities and its possibilities. Secondly, bad situational experiences will bring you closer to your loved ones. When we get into careless predicaments that are difficult to solve at first, we turn all of our attention and energies to those whom we love and cherish dearly. We look to them as a guiding light to bail us out of such tight jams. We do so because we presume they have the knowledge and foresight to avoid such precarious ones. Thirdly, we have to look at this thing objectively and subjectively. If one were in a similar predicament, then one can say that this thing is objective. And how they react to their happenings is subjective. Each one would respond to it in a different way. Fourthly, maintaining a healthy outlook over any uncertain condition is very vital to the mind, body, and soul. It is always best to remain calm and normal in whatever situational crisis you're going through. (I will discuss an attitude change at length in one of the subsequent chapters). Many of us tend to throw up the white flag when such adversarial experiences come our way. Many of us don't know how to rebound from such negativity. We can't let our statuses bully us into calling it quits. If something is broke but fixable, then fix it. Otherwise, let it run its course. Keeping a right attitude will justify your means to your solution in solving whatever situation you're going through. Lastly, we have no control over what will come. If we are here today, we could be gone that same day.

Sometimes, by committing acts of terrorism, such as the 9/11 tragedy, political leaders getting assassinated, mall killings, restaurant killings, terroristic threats, or school shootings, will only draw us closer to each other for a specific reason. There is some good in the most incorrigible person on this planet. And there is some good in your telling personal experiences to grow from. Concerning mine, I realize that we all have some difficult days to deal with. I look back at the bad situations I was presented with. I am thankful now that they are "water under the bridge." Such was my lot.

Rule 11: *To make the best out of a bad situation is to learn from it, grow from it, and move on.*

TWELVE
MISTREATMENT

Samuel Clark is a good friend of mine. He has worked in the police department of Newark, New Jersey, for more than twenty-five years. He is a former police lieutenant and a veteran police officer. Sam shares with us his insight that the police can be as incorrigible as these hardcore criminals. During his tenure as a cop, he has experienced widespread corruption in Newark's police department. Sam, along with politicians from all levels, a county prosecutor, a state and national attorney general, and the FBI presented documentary evidences of serious police corruption. However, elected officials and government law enforcement agencies ignored the complaints and evidences from around thirty police officers. Why did they do so? No one knows for sure. Consequently, of all of these chaoses, misunderstandings, and mishaps spurred Sam to write a book called *Total Misconduct*, to give his fair, accurate, and detailed accounts of his personal affairs with other crooked officers, while in duty. He has allowed me to highlight certain excerpts from the first chapter of his book. And these are some of his excerpts and analysis of what really happened:

It was a typical, hot Fourth of July holiday for Sam. He was ready to go home, eagerly waiting to join his family for a quiet celebration. In the police business, working is the norm. After finishing his paperwork, Sam was ready to leave. (Sam felt that if he had any indication of the misadventures that would change his life on that uneventful day, then he would have stayed in the office a few more hours. He didn't, and, accordingly, it made a negative impact on his life forever.) He encountered this traumatic experience. When he left the parking lot, he was heading to his destination. He had assumed that everything was normal. It was normal, until he noticed an ambulance and another police car thirty feet away from the ambulance. Sam noticed that the paramedics were putting the patient in the ambulance. He also noticed one of his fellow officers, Kevin Jones. Jones was there, interviewing one of the drivers involved in the accident. But he didn't want to distract him.

Assuming everything was all right, Sam proceeded to drive off to his destination in his personal car. Suddenly, he heard Officer Jones's voice come over the police radio. His voice was filled with excitement when he yelled, "Unit 231, give me the air." Sam reached and turned up his portable hand radio to find out what was going on. Sam thought he had better pull over to see if everything was normal. Again, Officer Kevin Jones's voice came over the police radio. Then another police officer's voice came over the radio, wanting to know his exact location. But Jones did not respond. When he didn't respond, the police dispatcher announced, "All units in the north, we have an assist officer at Central Avenue and West Market Street." Other police officers were riding to the aid of Officer Jones to see if he was in trouble. Even Sam came over because he wasn't that far away. Sam made a U-turn to help his fellow officer. But it wasn't one that he regretted because it unraveled his troubles.

By the time he reached that particular intersection, no strange activities were happening. The ambulance was gone. Officer Jones's marked car disappeared. The vehicle involved in the accident was gone. And not one single person was around. Still, Sam's careful vigilance made him suspicious of any mysterious activities that might have unfolded at that particular spot. Nothing happened, until he noticed a white four-door car just off of the middle of the avenue, about one hundred feet from the intersection. He noticed that four young males were standing along the passenger side of the car with their hands placed on the white car. And at each end of the car were two uniformed officers. Both officers were examining the young men. However, Sam didn't notice a patch on either of the officer's dark-blue uniform. Clark concluded that they couldn't have been Newark cops because both patches were on both sleeves near the shoulder and are highly visible. Sam thought they were campus police.

Sam noticed that the two young men, who were not being examined by the officers, took their hands off the white car and faced each other. The cops said something to them, and they both put their hands on the car. This feat was repeated around three or four more times, until Sam got out of his car to help them. As he got out, he noticed two Newark police officers in full uniform get out of a marked police car parked about twenty feet behind his but in the middle of the street. But Sam disregarded them, focusing all of his attention on the four unknown males and the officers around the white car. As he walked faster to see what the incident was about, he saw two of the men grab and grapple each other. Sam sensed that this commotion could get out of hand and become nasty and ugly. He intervened to break things up. But before he knew it, someone grabbed him from behind and was strangling him by the throat.

To make a long story short, Sam noticed two cops behind him. Both were reluctant to take the perpetrator off of him. Sam Clark mused to himself that there were other perpetrators involved. In any case, the suspect was choking Sam harder by now. He was choking him so hard that he nearly cut off his air supply. Sam was wondering why the other cops, who stood only a few feet away, were slow to react. With a concerted effort, Sam turned his head slightly to see who the guy was. What he saw sent shock waves throughout his body. To his astonishment, this perpetrator happened to be a Newark police officer himself. There you have it.

There must have been a reason why a cop was choking his fellow cop. To add insult to injury, the corrupt cop had threatened Sam with profanity. Still, Sam was wondering why the other cops did not stop this nut of a cop. All he could do at that moment was hope for a miracle. And a miracle did occur. The unknown officer let go of him. Sam turned and shouted, "I'm a f——king cop!" He showed his badge to the dirty cop. The cop apologized to Sam for his gross misconduct.

Dirty, stunned, dazed, and upset, Sam tried to talk to the other officers who had witnessed what happened. But the cops were apathetic and disinterested. When Sam began to come to his senses, he went to their precinct to file a report against this crazy cop. He found out that his name was Nathan De Barlow, who happened to work out of that precinct. Sam wrote him up for his inappropriate actions. After filing his reports, Sam was ready to leave for the hospital. Suddenly, he received a phone call from another officer, wanting to show him something. Lieutenant Polerri showed Sam a copy of De Barlow's report on what happened at that specific intersection. It was not what Sam had described what happened to him. The crooked cop told an outrageous lie. De Barlow's report contradicted Sam's report. De Barlow said Sam was swinging his arms wildly while approaching his partner from the rear. Sam's arguments were that the cop had a strong choke hold on his neck. To make matters worse, Sam learned that Lieutenant Polerri was part of the conspiracy to have him terminated.[3]

One bad cop used excessive force on a good cop, who did nothing wrong. The nasty cop could have killed him, but he didn't. Other cops observed what happened but were slow to react. Moreover, the aggressive cop wrote a dirty lie for his misdeeds. These were some of the liabilities that Samuel Clark, a veteran police officer himself, had to sustain to protect his civil rights. This

---

[3] Clark, Total Misconduct, 14–25.

is an unforgettable experience that would alter the destination of his career, shatter his belief in the fairness of law enforcement and the criminal justice system, and, most notably, change his life forever. Clearly, this was a case of police brutality. Clearly, this was a setup. And clearly, this was a case of gross mistreatment. To get the whole story, pick up a copy of his book.

Slavery is morally wrong, no matter what one's race, ethnicity, background, or creed is. It is unjust to take your fellow man and hold him in bondage. It is a fallacy to practice this servitude because one man's way of living is worlds apart from another person's. But such were the beliefs of certain countries at one time in this present world. As recorded in the annuals of time, Portugal, not Egypt, was the first-ever country to practice this precept. But long before the slave trade began, the Egyptians' perspective of slavery was, beyond question, different from other slaveholding nations and the United States. Slavery evolved out of her system by warfare. Any persons who were not killed or conquered from any invasion were taken in as prisoners of war and were made slaves. These persons were put into bondage to "get things done." My point is that when Egypt was ruling over the world with her powerful dynasties, she employed slaves to build her pyramids and the other startling wonders of the world. They were forced to work to survive. Her slaves were not flagellated, eaten, or killed at will. They were taken care of, despite being denied freedom, until another country overthrew Egypt. Otherwise, they would remain slaves, until death delivered them from serfdom. Her slave masters would treat them as such. When I go grocery shopping and see a product on the shelf that I like, I buy it. If I don't like it, I leave it alone. The point is, if they were sick or if the work was too demanding, the Egyptians nursed them back to their proper health or found them a task that was easier to perform. Such was Egypt's norm back in those days.

As for America, it's another story. We all know how slaves were treated. This system was cruel, barbaric, and dehumanizing.

Slaves were put up at auctions on the Virginia shorelines, like a commodity labeled with a price tag. Any slave, who rebelled or disobeyed their owner, was immediately put to death at the discretion of their slave masters. More so, animals were given preference over the slaves. While experiencing life as a free man, Frederick Douglas was passing through the state of Ohio. Depleted and hungry, he stopped for a meal to replenish. He noticed that the horses were fed first. Angrily, Douglass and his friends had to comply. They had to eat the remains from the plates of someone else's. As part of their learning experiences, most slaves had to emancipate and educate themselves.

If you think our system was brutal and inhumane, think again. The reason I say so is because Brazil's system was nearly three times as bad as ours or other parts of the world. She really took servitude to another level. Being the last of the Americas to do away with it, her slaves had rough working conditions. They were so rough, many fled from their owners' plantations. She placed her slaves deep in the Amazon, where it was extremely hot and sultry. Brazil practiced plantation exploitation. She placed slaves on sugarcane fields to produce sugar. Slaves used hoes to dig large trenches. But her working conditions were so unbearable that it resulted in certain deaths for her slaves. It is, also, understood that any slave she didn't like, she would put to death and consume for food. Nowadays, this is considered an act of cannibalism. Slaves she did like, she spared their lives for her well-being. Brazil's system was equated to medieval torture. She ended slavery in1888. But that didn't end her problem. Slaves, or any other person of African descent, were treated with horrible living conditions, like those in America. Their conditions were squalid, neglected, and dirty, sometimes resulting in certain diseases. Such an act was horrible and beastlike. Such mentality is a basic example of a glaring maltreatment.

A Successful Formula

Is our Judicial System a Fair One?

He will undoubtedly go down as America's most controversial intriguing sports figure. This former football player ran his way into the Football Hall-of-Fame and into our hearts, with his electrifying runs and impressive numbers on the grid iron. More so, he made a litany of television commercials and guest appearances, and films, living off his past glory. Who is this unique person I'm talking about? He goes by the name of Orental James Simpson. But he is commonly referred to as O. J. Simpson. Simpson is now running a new kind of run—he is running away from the law. It appears he keeps having run-ins with law officials. It is presumed he doesn't know how to stay out of trouble. In June of 1994, Simpson was accused of two counts of gruesome murder on his estranged wife, Nicole brown Simpson, and her estranged lover, Ronald Goldman. To make a long story short, it took the jury fifteen months to deliberate on his verdict. He was found not guilty on two counts of first degree murder.

Exactly thirteen years later, after the jury acquitted him, O. J. Simpson is tried for another felony. He and his co-accuser, Charles "C. J." Stewart, are found guilty of twelve robbery, kidnapping, and weapons charges, following a run-in with a pair of sports memorabilia dealers he had the previous year. Currently, both are serving jail terms which could carry a possible life term with no parole for them in five years. On October 4th, 2008, the jury delivered their verdicts to Simpson and Stewart. Both were found guilty. The jury consisted of a predominately white and female jury. It took them fourteen hours to reach a unanimous decision.

Do you think our judicial system is a fair and just one? I ask because many believe that the decision to incarcerate Simpson, based on his testimonies, was biased as a carryover from his previous verdict. According to Simpson's lawyer, Yale Galanter and Gabriel Grasso, Galanter felt all along that the jury would find him guilty. Grasso reasoned that the verdict's and sentences were excessive. He felt that if the former football player had walked into a bank with an AK-47 assault rifle, robbed it, and duct taped the people inside, Simpson would have received an equally stiff sentence.

Is America's justice scale an unbalanced one, favoring whomever, based on race, religion, sex, or the status quo? This will undeniably be an open question for many incoming years to debate. It is a thought provoking question to consider and reconsider. Years from now, you can debate yourselves as to whether Simpson did or did not commit such atrocious crimes. Or was he set up by the hotel's security cameras to steal these sports accessories, for his intent? All of these strong supporting arguments point to the fact that they are open for discussion on your perspective on what is fair or not fair.

At the same time, our legal system can be quite objective. We have repeated offenders who feel they can take matters into their own hands. And the bad are trying to take control of the streets. But when is enough is enough? Again, this is a reasonable question for anyone to ask. These miscreants may have to be behind bars for awhile, until they decide to become law-abiding citizens and ultimately turn away from their perverse and stubborn ways. I'll admit! The law is the law and there are ground rules and regulations in which all have to abide. The bad want control of the streets. We cannot let this happen. It's very easy for one to get out of line; it's very difficult to put one back in one's proper place. Bear this thought in mind: no one, no one is above the law, written the law, or, as a matter of fact, invented the laws for their purpose.

Mistreatment, depending on how you view it, whether you can accept it or not, are another drawback of life we have to contend with, unfortunately. No one, despite one's race, ethnicity, or gender, deserves to be treated in a foul fashion. Because one group of people cannot accept another's cultures, ideas, or beliefs, it is not reason enough to treat them with unfairness. It may be another way of saying we discriminate against those we oppose.

Despite our irreconcilable, petty, insecure differences, no one should ever feel they are superior or inferior to those whom they deal with on a daily basis. Still, to this present day, racism is institutionalized in this great country and in some parts of the world. And it is institutionalized within the black community. Whatever, we have to overcome this conundrum and proceeded in the manner we were intended for. When we wake up in the morning, we put our clothes on the same way. And when we lay down at night, we take them off like everyone else.

Concerning the aftereffects of Hurricane Katrina, a politician was interviewed on television. She pointed out an interesting observation in its aftermath. She cited that water doesn't discriminate against homes. The reason she said so was because millionaires' homes were ransacked as well as poor peoples' homes. She was fighting for financial aid from Congress to get the city back on its feet. If water or the other elements don't discriminate, then why do we?

The great Leon Sullivan was an aggressive, influential clergyman, who championed for civil rights of African-Americans in Philadelphia and elsewhere. He worked out of Zion Baptist Church. He was a strong and vocal leader, who refused to let the wrongs overtake the rights. Very well liked and well respected, his church congregation labeled him "the lion of Zion." He once brought up an interesting observation concerning unfairness. His main point was, in today's society, blacks are destroying other blacks at an alarming rate, since whites have killed off blacks, before slaves were emancipated. It is another sad statistics, unfortunately. To be more specific, this one fact can be contributed to gang killing, women, getting ahead in life, or just plain jealousy. He reasoned that blacks are the most jealous race of people he encountered on this planet. For example, certain blacks, because of the color of their skin or any other physical characteristic, would treat other blacks, who don't measure up to their standard of living, as inferior. He, also, pointed out that when he grew up in the old South, he experienced wide-open prejudice from whites. For instance, if a white person saw a black person walking on the same sidewalk, then he thinks that the ground is cursed. Such distorted notions, back in those days, are, now, considered a myth and are obsolete. Nowadays, the black community in general is casting out unfairness upon each other, thanks to our minor differences. These ill treatments of others have got to subside. When we want a personal favor from others, we know how to charm them to get it. But when we want them to stay clear of our paths, we treat them like they are nobodies or with some hostility. This is very wrong, indeed! We should all stop rushing to judgment so quickly because of our personal dislikes. Treat others like you would want them to treat you.

Stop going around telling others you don't like them. It's safe to say you like them but not their elements-their thoughts, their actions, their attitudes, and their mannerisms. Nonetheless, you like them for who they are and what they stand for. Always treat others with proper respect, dignity, class, and fairness they deserve. You'll never know when you'll need a big, big favor from that distinct person. Always keep your channels of communications actively flowing to others who surround you. If someone dislikes you, overlook him and keep going. Otherwise, treat everyone in a like manner.

Rule 12: *Remember, how you treat others will come back to you tenfold.*

THIRTEEN
THE BOY WHO COULD

You are nearing the end of this book. And as you do, I hope you have applied all there is I have written thus far. But before closing, I want you as my reader to have some fun. In this one chapter alone, I will attempt to intersperse poetry with reality. We face real-life situations everyday in every phase of society. The crux of this chapter is about having some deep faith in all of your doings. It's all about believing in oneself, despite some nasty falls, road barriers, or what others are saying. Humans will take aim at what you're doing for the betterment of your life, criticize you to the fourth degree, and try to make you their scapegoat, if you let them. One thing is certain: they cannot live for you or take your place in history. A person's ability to seek real happiness comes from within. And it is strictly up to you to put a premium on things that you desire. To unravel your hidden talents and be amazed at what you can accomplish speaks highly in and of itself. As a child growing up, I was taught to never take your abilities for granted. Always believe in yourself, whether you're at work or at play. For instance, if my friends and I wanted to convene over a game of baseball or basketball, we played our hearts out until the very end just to win. It was like we were busting our butts off to make it to the pros. Even in our chores and studies, we went to the ends of the earth just to put the finishing label on our assignments or earn a decent grade. This type of motivation was old school. It was deeply embedded in our bloodstreams. We didn't need any motivational classes or readings to give ourselves a shot in our rear ends to get going. We observed and picked up on what others around us were doing. We took care of and took pride in our doings. This kind of learning helped mold me into the unique individual I am today.

And that is why I am writing about a fictitious, little twelve-year-old boy in verse form, who possessed the maturity, savvy, and credentials of any mature individual trying to master his goals. He possessed all of the mental discipline and desire to put the finishing touches on his project in life. These are the poems I wrote to further illustrate my points.

> This is a poem about a little boy, who goes by the name of Todd,
> Who had his fair share of skeptics and critics, as if to say he was against all odds.
> Society labeled him a mishap by using discouraging words.
> They did this to see if he would be dissuaded.
> Because he refused to let that dampen his spirit,
> he fought on anyhow, so they would be persuaded.

True to its nature, society will heap its negativity, guilt, and pessimism upon you, if you are not strong enough to stand up against its repercussions. Society will say all kinds of things to discourage you. But Todd refused to give in to such foolishness. He had alligator skin to ward off any abusive remarks directed at him. It may have seemed like the whole world was against him. But he didn't quit because he knew he had the capability to get things done. No miracle worker was he. He was an ordinary guy with ordinary standards going about his chores the best way he knew how. Todd knew that once he gave in, then others around him would give up on him just as well. He refused to bow down to their demands.

> Todd didn't care how people felt or what they
> thought.
> It didn't matter who was wrong or right.
> From all of this he drew inner strength, making
> him press on no matter what with all his might.

Todd grew immune to what others around him were saying. He became indifferent to rumors, gossips, lies, and heresies from anyone. Todd knew very well that people would throw all kinds of obstacles and road barriers your way to throw you off your course in attaining greatness. By listening to his pessimists, the only remedy he showed them was to try a little harder. His philosophy was it did not matter who was right or wrong but was what was right and wrong. People have a twisted way of thinking. All of us hypothesize with our different rules and regulations on what is and what isn't. But Todd stuck to his guns. He stuck to one rule. It was a rule that was for everybody to see, not just for specific individuals.

> Todd's tactics disagreed with his fellow observers,
> as they were overtaken more with doubt.
> But he kept up his faith anyway,
> be they direct or roundabout.

We have our own unique way of putting the finishing touches on a project. Some will agree or disagree, depending on your method. It can be hard to try to get everybody on the same page in accomplishing one's desires. So were Todd's intentions. He knew some were either for or against him. He knew some were not going to see things from his perspective. But he ignored them, dug down deep within his limits, searched for his inner voice, and then proceeded as usual. He was out to prove that he was neither physically nor mentally incapable. Sometimes, people may not agree with your methods of getting your main point across to others. However, as time moves on, they soon get the scope as to why you chose the path you took.

> Todd went to an extreme to silence his observers.
> He did this to be well-justified.
> This gave him an inner joy to master his feat, to
> be honored, pleased, appreciated, and glorified.

This particular stanza is something to think about. This young lion went to an extreme to quiet his doubters. He may have been somewhat physically exhausted. But in any case, he persevered, until his task was done. And before moving on to the next phase of his life, he wanted everyone to know that he was most justified. And he was at peace with himself. Todd knew all along that he had a determined faith that would see him through any difficult situation or triumph over any adversity. Faith is one of the components that will erase the seeds of gloominess, despair, and self-doubt. Todd possessed the qualities of hope, promise, prosperity, and optimism in making it in this, oftentimes, antagonistic world. His assets would help him overcome any challenging situations he faced. He showed them all where they were wrong in underestimating him. Positive forces enabled him to eradicate his obstacles.

> To say what he could not based on their beliefs
> would be an unfair statement of his true abilities.
> It would.
> But he showed them all where they were wrong,
> proving, after all, he was the little boy who could.

One of our major faults is we often read into another person's demeanor the wrong way. We probably sized him up wrong or took him for granted. A lot of us are narrow-minded and biased in our judgment of others. Most of our preconceived notions about others are way off base. For instance, when a player is drafted,

A Successful Formula

he may be slightly underrated in evaluating his talent. Bear in mind that some of these cast-off sport players are Hall of Famers today. In the 1960s, an ordinary running back for the Washington Redskins by the name of Charley Taylor was drafted. No weighty draft choice was he. He was just your average tailback by football standards. And he turned out to be an average back, putting up average numbers in his prime. As time went by, he was not putting up any impressive numbers for his team at that position. One day, his coach decided to try him in a new position, rather than trade him or cut him. He switched him to wide receiver. Charley earned his birth in professional football's Hall of Fame. My point is central in not doubting anyone, based on your unfair analysis of another's ability. You'll never know what the deck of cards has in store for you. My made-up character, Todd, is a great example of what I'm talking about. He turned a deaf ear and ignored all of those disbelievers surrounding him. He warded off their vitriolic comments and negative thinking. He listened to his subconscious and gained amazing results. In the long haul, he gained their respect and admiration. Todd showed them what true faith was all about and what wonders it will do for you, if you believe in your credentials. And he earned a special place in their hearts. Maybe Todd may have appeared as an underachiever, but in the final analysis, he triumphed and prevailed over his worst skeptics and critics.

To believe in yourself is one of the greatest assets you can have going for you. You can envision as to what lies ahead in your true realm of possibilities. A person's mental capability to see things beyond the imagination that no one else can envision is an amazing blessing. Many times over, people will form their one-sided, biased opinions about you knowing the true story. They may form their subjective opinions without weighing in all of the facts. Nine times out of ten, opinions are formed based on the facts of our disapproval of that person. They are subjective more so than objective. They are neither right nor wrong only good, bad, or indifferent. Only a handful of people will have that uncanny ability to change nonbelievers into believers. Whatever means you employ will show even the worst skeptic that you can do anything once you release all of your positive forces, reach back, and bring your components into fruition. Your subconscious mind will tell you that you have unlimited faith to believe whatever the mind can conceive. You can convert your negatives into positives. Even you will be amazed at what you have mastered. The mind is a powerful tool in and of itself. It will give you the strength to believe that you can triumph over any difficulty or adversity that arises. Never take your talents or yourself for granted. You don't have to sell yourself short or come up on the short end to make a strong impression just to please others. Believe in your worthwhile accomplishments because your abilities to grasp the intangibles are only seconds away.

Todd may have been that dark horse that no one anticipated would rise to the occasion. He overlooked his liabilities, limits, and despairs in maintaining his levelheadedness and in pursuing his dreams. It seemed like the whole world was coming at him. Todd dug down deep within himself, listening to that distant inner voice, telling him he could triumph over his failures. Ultimately, Todd steered himself in the right direction. He took them on anyhow, took things in stride, withstood his critics, ignored his naysayers, and persevered, until the last struggle was conquered. He stood tall against all odds, proving that he was the "little boy who could."

Rule 13: *In-depth faith always wins over difficulties.*

FOURTEEN
AN ATTITUDE WITH LATITUDE

A radio deejay once talked about adjusting your attitude for the five o'clock rush hour going home. What he meant was you had plenty of zest and limitless energy leaving your jobs. That's fine! But what about going to work in the morning or preparing for your day's schedule? What kind of attitude are you on then? Are you on one that is laissez-faire or enthusiastic? Are you on one that projects a self-defeatist mentality as a carryover from the previous day or a new one filled with gratitude? These are tough questions to consider. Regardless of what time of the day it is, what day of the week it is, what week of the month it is, or what month of the year it is, your attitude should always be one of cheerfulness and optimism. We live in a world that is full of ups and downs. The minute we came into existence, we were not guaranteed a gold credit card or a gold plate with our names engraved on it. Instead, we were dealt with an abundance of adversities, mishaps, setbacks, and other negatives to overcome. But we could not have achieved greatness had we taken on a sullen spirit. Picture a child at an amusement park or a seashore setting. He exhibits a picture-perfect, happy-go-lucky, carefree mentality. He runs around with other children in a sportive manner. At that moment, he is in a world where all problems or heaviness are nonexistent. He projects an image that he doesn't have the slightest care or concern in the world. He goes about in his customary procedure of eating his hot dog, ice cream, or cotton candy. If something traumatic were to happen in his presence, he would not let that dampen his spirit. He has no worries, responsibilities, burdens, or problems associated with his mind-set. His disposition is always of the same nature. To paraphrase what I'm saying his attitude has plenty of latitude.

As for you and me, we should be on the same page as these unconcerned children. I know it is easier said than done and there are a lot of factors to consider, but we should lead by example. As mature, full-grown citizens, we should always exemplify our points of view with hope and promise, no matter how bleak things may seem at the present moment. Taking an overdose of aspirin or committing some form of suicide is no well-defined, definitive solution to fixing something that is non-fixable. And to start the day off on a sour note will only make matters worse. The attitude you reveal to others will determine the type of person you will become for the rest of your life. And I would hope that it is one that will gain you friends and lessen your enemies. In theory, your attitude is your life. And wherever you go and whatever you do, it should always be one of optimism and hope, one that has an abundance of latitude. The word latitude means having tolerance and freedom of choice over anything. That means you should free yourself from self-doubt, self-pity, pessimism, negativity, or any other guiltiness associated with this word.

The one that sticks out is why do we act out in the manner of a spoiled child from time to time? What are our rationales for revealing such out- of-the-way attitudes around those we come in contact with on a daily basis? Could we blame it on our relationship with our family members? Does the work pressure allow us to go off with some unexplained, irrational behavior? Could it be peer pressure from those we socialize with? We tend to act out of frustration, resentment, nervousness, anxiety, and fear from unfortunate situations. To project a demoralizing spirit is an unhealthy way of living. Also, it can hurt your mind and body as well. Nobody in this tough, crazy world is in love with you or is going to give you anything for your benefit. But does that mean we should go around mulling all day over our failures? Not at all! Regardless of the outcomes, we should look at the sunny side of life with plenty of zest, enthusiasm, and promise no matter how many setbacks or mishaps we endure. To take the wrong attitude is like pouncing down on someone who is already at the bottom of the barrel. Taking this outlook is very wrong and degrading. There are many times we have to overcome such adversities to get around these trying situations. And applying the right attitude is your best remedy. There are many negative attitudes to consider and most noteworthy of all is worrying.

It's no use fretting or sitting around, moping over something you have no control over. Many of us do but for no apparent reason. If you do, you start to worry yourself into a chronic condition. And it's very unhealthy and unwise to the mind and spirit. Your mind doesn't function properly. You cannot think things out clearly and rationally. You lose some of your motivational juices flowing from your inner conscience. You deprive your body of the proper nourishment and rest it needs to function. Lack of good sleep will affect your mental outlook somewhat. And you wake up in a sour mood. To think about what has transpired the day before will ruin your days and chores. You have to make some adjustments to decrease your worrying and increase your living. Life is full of highs and lows, but to worry over things that are trite and irrelevant is a not good.

What I am talking about is an attitude adjustment. I'm talking about the messages people say to themselves and how they feel about certain things. People should become more aware of the messages they say to themselves and how it makes them feel. For example, concerning jealousy, if I was in a relationship with a lady and she leaves me for another man, then I would probably feel that I'm a real loser. If I wasn't a real loser then she will still be with me. I may feel a little jealous or depressed. However, if I'd say that, if it's her loss then I will really feel bad about it. But then she's losing out. I may have more energy and feel better about myself in attitudinal changes; the initial step is becoming aware of what a message is saying to me. How I want this message to be grasped is my choice to make.

Moodiness and depression are not the same. Depression is different for different people. Some people are clinically depressed. Depression is associated with reduced levels of a neurotransmitter called serotonin. When levels of serotonin are too low, the brain and the rest of your body can't respond as fast it should. It seems like the world is against you. And your ability to handle it is slightly handicapped. It's a chemical reaction in the body and people suffering from it will need medication to help them feel better. Someone who is always moody or ornery on a daily basis may be having just a terrible day. It may be that something happened that they have no control over. It does not need treatment. They may need some support for other kinds of things, but it's not a life view. It's more of a situational and a state- of-mind thing. If someone were frequently moody, then it would be a concern, if it works against that person. If one walks into a job everyday and one is in a bad mood, then no one will interact with him. They can't get things done based on the fact that people won't cooperate with him. Because of the fact that that person is foul to be around with, his moodiness is working against him. That person needs to change his approach and figure out how he's going to change their approach, meaning those he alienated against him. Let's assume that I am a writer, writing something in my house. I am alone. I am not interacting with people. Then I feel better by being by myself. I may be in a bad mood. If I am going to let myself be in a foul mood and it doesn't have an impact on anyone, then I will feel better because it gives me permission to feel foul and it's working for me. There is no reason for me to change it. But if it interferes with my relationship with my wife, husband, or children and I am still acting out in a negative way and my spouse says that I am miserable, then it stops working for me. I need to do something to change this because it's not working for me. And when somebody gets to the point when they are ready to commit suicide, then it's got a chemical base to it. They may need medication, treatment, or whatever. This has gone from a reaction to what is around them to an actual mental illness. Life is full of tough times. One can't go through life without depression, stress, sadness, or grief because in life, things don't always work out for your benefit. It's how you move through it. Actually, depression can be a gift because it can tell you that things are not working right. I need to make a change. And you use that as an impetus to move your life in a different direction and that might be the direction for you to go. It is when people get stuck in it and unable to move out of it that it becomes a problem. And when someone starts feeling very sad and feels that life is not worth living then they need professional intervention. Depression has a few meanings. When someone is mildly depressed, he feels sad for himself and his environment. But one is really depressed when he is down and out. He needs medical treatment.

Consider this thought: arrogance, cockiness, and masochism are very foul attitudes to live with. Usually, those who take such unenviable measures always wind up alienating those who they are in daily contact with. Those who reveal such faulty pride, most likely, are gang or mob members. There is no logical explanation, to this very day, why a group of men from one section of the city will look down on another group from a different section because they won't go along with their program. All of this boils down to who has a superiority complex. Again, taking this approach is erroneous, due to the fact that a lot of people are extremely sensitive. They go around carrying their feelings on their sleeves. And this deflates their egos, bruises their prides, add to their grudges, and hurt their feelings. As a result of all of this, they turn to domestic violence to convey their point. Mob members, likewise, play a major role in this respect. They crave for money, power, and prestige, and they do this by ridiculing each other with bullets. Many will destroy one another over family matters and inheritances. They have no values and have no aim to become anything worthwhile in life, and they lack education. They don't want to work for a living. If you are a gang or mob member, all of this negative living starts with the home life. They have no goals to be anything. They are jobless. To go out into the world and prey on the innocent is a faux pas, by all accounts. This negative attitude soon catches up to them the law penalizing them to the fullest extent. Such a mentality only will bring you troubles, not triumphs in the long run.

The Rio Carnafest is known to be the wildest celebration of its kind anywhere in the world and, supposedly, the largest celebration in the world. With all of the color, glamour, glitter, and pageantry associated with it, this carnival is really a magnificent sight to behold. I just love how the thousands of parade participants line up, almost in a vicinity of about five miles, with their sea of different colors, eagerly waiting to kick off a wild, jubilant, merrymaking event and send the raucous crowd into frenzy. The way these Brazilians line up and march like army soldiers to the tune of their music reminds one of a New Year's Day parade.

How this parade operates is that the best of the dancers are chosen from the best. In others words, the judges have already decided who comes first, second, third, and so on. Whichever group has the best dance steps and costume designs are declared the winner. These marchers and their exotic costumes light up the Brazilian nightlife and their fans. And what's so amazing about this revelry is it kicks off its celebration from midnight to sunrise. Most of us are already in bed at these hours. But for these avid partygoers, they are still celebrating when the sun is ready to crack the night sky. I, also, noticed that it is a Brazilian tradition to project a worry-free, happy-go-lucky, and responsibility-free attitude. To them, it is almost second nature. In his perspective, the problems in his world are only miniscule. He symbolizes an almost picturesque, carefree attitude. He doesn't let his troubles bully him into a panic. His burdens are almost to the point where they are nonexistent. To the average Brazilian, he is truly amazing of how he keeps his cultural heritage with so little formal education and minimal work ethics. He'll dance his problems away. And he projects an attitude with plenty of latitude.

By the same token, about two hours north of Rio de Janeiro, by flight, is a close-knit community called Salvador de Bahia, a remote little city. This private place for citizens is similar to the Cape Cod community. And to its citizens, their motto is "one day at a time." Another way of saying it is they're only concerned with problems, problems that may confront them at the present moment. Yesterday is irrelevant because they have no control over what transpired in the past. They don't worry about tomorrow because tomorrow is not a promise to them, and it can take care of itself. Their chief concern is about what happens today. And what's even more important is how they approach their dilemmas. Their attitude is one of relaxation, no worries, no cares, no mishaps, and so on. It's one of letting tomorrow take care of itself. They won't permit the pressures of the world to defeat them in their peregrinations. They define an attitude that has no concerns, quandaries, or any high-strung characters. The present is all that matters. Taking one day at a time is their theory. To this native Brazilian, his mental outlook is hospitable and phlegmatic. If an air raid were about to hit his city, he would not become distraught, until it actually happened. Nothing could ever push his panic buttons because he won't allow that to happen. To him, he paints an attitude that is nearly paradise-like. He wants to be in a relaxed mode when he wakes up in the morning. Dealing with the present is his primary concern. He'll worry about tomorrow when it arrives.

Those who proclaim to have superiority over others are once again overrun with a repulsive attitude aimed at another group of people. To literally wake up and feel that you are better than your fellow man is wrong. Haven't you dealt with people who think that in many ways they are far better than you? Perhaps, more so on their terms. But in true fashion, they are not. Some may make you believe that because they have plenty going for them, but it doesn't make them in any way, shape, or form different from you at all. The foods you eat, the beverages you drink, or the jobs you have will not make you the great person you perceive yourself to be. For instance, a Wall Street broker is no better than a salesperson or even a street sweeper for that matter. One may sit at his desk and watch the numbers change every five minutes to up their shares in stock. Or one may have to hit the pavements, going from door to door, to meet his monthly sales quota just to earn a decent paycheck. But at the end of the day, regardless of what our job titles are, we all have to lay down the same way like everybody else. There are those that reside in different sections of cities, who feel like they are far superior then someone else. Maybe, one person can afford a luxurious, spacious home. Then again, he still has to hit the workforce to pay off his bills, mortgages, or rents.

Doctor Sullivan once remarked to his church congregation that blacks in certain Philadelphia neighborhoods look down upon blacks from other sections because they live in different areas. He sensed that the black community was a house divided, which could not stand. He further elaborated on the fact that certain blacks dwelling in certain sections with incomes far greater than the average blacks were no different in this sense than other African-Americans residing in low-income areas. He wanted to emphasize the fact that those blacks that were moving up to a better lifestyle should not feel they were superior to blacks who got by barely. And don't forget your roots and how you got started. His argument was that the black community still has some in-house cleaning to do to progress as a race of people. Despite our irreconcilable differences, Sullivan felt that we are still in the same boat. He sensed that blacks were quick to pull down other blacks because they didn't want to see certain blacks get ahead of them in their careers. We were like crabs in a barrel. When one crab sees another crab trying to climb out, the other crab pulls him down. Perhaps, one is more versatile in his capacity, but that does not give him the privilege to view him as inferior, because his standards of living aren't on the same level as his. This is definitely the wrong approach—to pass judgment so quickly on others.

Lastly, we have some people who have serious mood swings. To this day, no one can figure out why some people tend to welcome you with open arms one day and pretend you don't exist the next day. One doesn't know if they had a bad night the night before, if something is on their mind, if they are going through some tough times, or if they are just plain uppity in their mannerisms. Again, it is unjust and unfair to presume that the person you deal with on a consistent basis is not on the same level as you are. Doctor Sullivan had plenty of inspirational sayings on climbing the ladder of success. One of them sticks out like a sore thumb. And it reads in italic words: *The same people you meet on the way up, you're going to meet on the way down*. Don't turn your back on your fellow man because your advantages may outweigh his limitations in nearly all aspects of life or you feel you are better than him in a lot of ways. These are definitely insulting attitudes to live by.

Your attitude should never be one that is difficult to switch around. You can adjust from a sour one to a good one. Always thank your Creator for waking and getting you up when you first open your eyes in the morning. Think about all of those people who are either handicapped or an invalid. Despite their physical limitations, they still have to project a positive mind-set to keep going. Any negative or wrong thinking associated with it should be cast away. Life is indeed very tough. But we have to persevere through the tough times to get to our ultimate destinations. You have to decide if you are going to progress from your current situation of feeling saturnine or remain stagnant. It will make you feel like the day has either eight or eighty hours. You must make that call. Whatever you do or wherever you go, the right kind of attitude will make you overcome many difficulties to obtain greatness, not deviate from it. Before closing out this chapter, I will leave you with a short verse on attitude changes.

> As if I hand you a roseate attitude, one that suits my needs,
> As if mine is full of gratitude,
> so shall you witness my good deeds.

You readjust your kitchen clocks to the different seasons of the year. You readjust your alarm clock to wake up in time for your day's busy schedule. So why not readjust your mentality to meet your life's work from season to season? There is no harm in that. Regardless of what time of the season it is, make sure your attitude is filled with plenty of latitude, free from any negativity or the public's backlash, to give you an optimistic and sunny outlook in your endeavors.

Rule 14: *Every morning, we choose what attitude will be ours for the day. What attitude will you choose tomorrow morning?*

FIFTEEN

PUSH

One of the most powerful tools we could have going for us is the all-encompassing word, *prayer*. Prayer can do more than just make drastic changes in one's life. It can do amazing wonders. It can unlock doors to a new way of living. It can unravel things that were never seen or heard of before. Even when it seems that we are in a hopeless, bleak situation, prayer can lift us out of an adverse situation. Prayer can convert the nonbeliever into a believer. That is why it is beneficial and essential to use prayer in every aspect of our lives. Without prayer, you will only see minor improvements in your endeavors. With prayer, you will see drastic improvements in your tasks. Most of the time, we have to "push" our way to accomplish anything that is meaningful. And prayer is an asset to guide us along our paths to greatness. The acronym I'm using for my title, P U S H, is not about Operation Push which you may be familiar with. It's a different one I'm using. It's priceless, economical, timeless, and affordable. It's in widespread use every day. It's in the four corners of this ungodly world. The acronym for it is "Pray, Until Something Happens." Always pray, until that something wonderful and miraculous experience happens to you. You're prayers are subjective, in the first place. They should always be unceasing. Always pray, until they are answered. And why don't you do just that?

What Is Prayer?

Prayer is a silent communication with God. It's acknowledging the Holy One, giving thanks to his loving mercy, his grace, his sovereignty, his majesty, and his goodness. It's giving thanks to him for all that he's done, continuing to do, and will continue do for the incoming years. Too many times, we overlook this essential tool to fix whatever problems arise in our lives. Instead, take matters into our own hands, feeling we can solve any conundrum without its assistance. We, as fellow beings, have a tendency to toss God aside, when we plan something for our benefit. We tend to forget the loving nature he has provided for us. He promised to never leave us or forget us. We have a strong tendency to bite our tongues, at times, but he never bites his. Never! Our Lord God is true to his words. If God says he's going to do something, then believe in your heart every word he says. In essence, prayer is realizing that God is still performing miracles in our lives. He means what he says. His existence is non experiential. Physically, we cannot see or feel the Invisible One, but we know that he is ever present because he works his wonders in mysterious ways, performing positive things that are both seen and unseen by the naked eye. Prayer is witnessing that God is with us, "in spirit and in truth." For instance, someone is lying in a hospital bed moribund, ready to pass on to another life—well, that same loving God will touch one in such a way that is hard to explain and imagine and make one whole again. Always use prayer as an instrument to whatever you're going through. Prayer is your channel of communication to God.

Why Pray?

Why should we pray? Because it gives us our daily guidance, confidence, insight, and strength for whatever circumstances we are going through. It enables us to stand up against the wiles of the world. Without prayer, we are lost, like a baby sheep that has left the flock and gone astray. We need to pray for the recycling and betterment of our well-beings. Since we are mortal, we need prayer as a source to help us polish up our strengths and strengthen our weaknesses. As I've stated earlier in one of my chapters on dealing with problems, prayer is an excellent antidote to solving problems that are unsolvable. Prayer can melt down even the most challenging problem imaginable, like melting a giant snowball into a puddle of water.

But why should we pray? We need to pray constantly for spiritual nourishment and for growth. Like a plant that needs watering for its vital minerals and vitamins, we need to be fed spiritually and stay with the Word to keep us motivated. And in addition, it is central to pray so that your will is aligned with the will of God. And did you ever notice that God answers our prayer requests in three different ways? Here is how they are answered:

1. *Yes!* If God says yes, then we know it's all right with his divine plans. When we pray to God and he says yes right off the bat, then we know that our will is consumed in his.

2. *Yes, but wait!* If God says those three words, it's because he feels that we're not ready for whatever he has in store for us at that particular moment. He wants us to be patient and have some more time to mature and gel us into whatever is going to happen.

3. *No!* If he says no, then it's for a specific reason. It isn't because he doesn't love us or want us to have it. More so, it's because he has something better in store for us. Since we are his marvelous creations, he knows us better than we know ourselves. And he knows what is better for our being. Like a good parent, who doesn't spoil his child, God operates the same way.

We pray to ask the Holy One to guide us on a daily basis and see what his will is for us on that distinct day. Prayer is our remedy to what ails us. Lastly, it is vital to pray and call on him during good times as well as bad times. Don't wait, until a world crisis happens or a bad, personal experience hits you in an unexpected way. God always yearns to help us, no matter what our circumstances are. Were you to take a preparatory test to get in an institution of higher learning, don't pray to God the night before you take the test. You should have been praying from day one up until that juncture to ask him to open up your mind so that you might achieve a high enough score. Always be consistent in your daily prayer requests because prayer is spiritual nourishment.

How Should We Pray?

In your daily prayer requests, you pray specifically for what you need. When you were a child and you asked for a favor from your parents, you were direct and straightforward in your asking. God expects us to be the exact same way with him when we ask him for a favor. I cannot speak for every Christian because of their beliefs. But I will say, in my upbringing, I was taught in my Bible studies that God will answer a laconic prayer much quicker than one that is verbosity. Why? Because the person who wants one thing at a time will receive it quicker than the one who wants the solar system. Our subjective prayers are answered, but they won't all come at once. All things are in God's time. He knows what our needs are but like a good parent, he won't spoil us. He is not on the same timetable as we are. God is never too early or too late. He is always on time. When we go to him in private and ask him for something, we must have patience and forbearance, before all of these worldly pleasures are added to our wish list. We are not in control of our own destinies. Christ Jesus is.

Since Jesus Christ is God incarnate, he stood on the riverbanks and taught his disciples and followers to pray to the One in heaven fast, before they did anything. And he instructed them to be concise and to believe in God, when they pray earnestly. And did you ever notice that Jesus Christ always prayed to his father, asking him specifically what his will was? Christ descended from his heavenly seat to come into this evil world to lead by example. And he led a perfect example in all his doings. He expects us to follow suit. Christ always prayed first, asking in faith what his duty was before he made a move. He expects us to follow suit in his patterns.

Since this is the very last chapter of this book, I strongly suggest that you use prayer as a fundamental building block to accomplish your dreams and aspirations in your respective endeavors. Prayer can do amazing wonders for you, if you open up your heart to God and give him a chance. God does not force himself on us. He sits back and patiently yearns for us to ask his help. Moreover, God does not dictate or bully us into doing something that is not our will. Rather, he is humble and he superintends us along our paths. He wants us to reciprocate his loving and generous mercy in a like manner. Summing up everything, prayer is a sound instrument that has been passed down from generation to generation to enable us to progress in our constant struggles in this ever-changing world. Whatever you do and wherever you go, always remember this golden rule: *Pray Until Something Happens.*

Rule 15: *Pray! There is immeasurable power in it.*

CONCLUSION

By the time you finish reading this manuscript, I hope that it opened up your eyes to the truth. I have provided some excellent examples, hoping to convey my message to every reader who reads this written work. It can be difficult to get everybody on the same page and to get things done. I thank you for taking time and applying some of my medicine to help heal your wounds from the abrasive tactics of society. I hope that the elements, which exemplify the sole, basic characteristics in this book, will enable you to use them as a tool to reinvent yourselves. Nothing worth achieving happens overnight. It comes with patience, hard work, time, foresight, determination, the right attitude, and of course, the all-powerful instrument, prayer. Without these basic mechanisms, one will never know what true success means. They may never reap the benefits of successful living. True success is not always measured in monetary gains, popularity, tangibles, or how high you climb your personal ladder for recognition. It's measured by helping others, seeing others happy, and how happy you are. Unfortunately, we all have skeletons in our closets to clean out. We all have another chance at redemption. Despite our current circumstances, we have to persevere, maintain a healthy attitude, overcome them to the best of our abilities, and proceed with our life's works. Each and every day we open our eyes, we are given a new beginning at something that is worthwhile to attain. Some things are meant to be for certain people. For others, it isn't. Each ethnic group brings to the table something unique, remarkable, and extraordinary, which are far beyond one's imagination to share with this world to make it a better place to reside in. Every generation was put here for a specific reason. We were put here to help America grow to an even greater nation beyond others. Were you to experience adverse situations, the only remedy for that is to learn from it and move on to the next phase of your lives. And were you to meet a stranger by happenstance, never tie his hands, because he deserve as much of a chance to reap the benefits in life as anyone else. Remember to choose your words, carefully and considerately, to help develop your interpersonal skills, when dealing with others. Above all else, stop discriminating against those whom we oppose just because our one-sided views are not aligned with theirs.

Just before signing off on his weekly Sunday morning radio broadcast, Reverend Al Sharpton comments about those who must work on their own weaknesses, before eliminating the weaknesses of others. He says that one must work on that person they see standing in front of their mirror, before leaving home. He further cites that a better person leads to a better family; a better family leads to a better neighborhood; a better neighborhood leads to a better community; a better community leads to a better nation; and a better nation leads to a better world.

Another friend once told me to always clean off your own doorsteps, before you clean off another's. Numerous people have paraphrased these proverbs. Basically, they're saying the same thing. And I adhere on these sound principles, in establishing a salubrious relationship among your fellow beings.

Whatever your form of happiness is, in applying these guiding principles can only help, not hinder you from achieving greatness. Some may have already written the text of their lives and some are just beginning. But many are in the commentary phase. I thank God He has allowed me to write this book and I hope it will touch one's life in a positive way. And I thank you in supporting it. May God bless you, always!

Final rule: *Your life is like a book. It's not the prologue or the epilogue that makes it attractive. It's the story between them that makes it attractive.*

BIBLIOGRAPHIES

Clark, Samuel. *Total Misconduct:* Disclosure, Research, and Publishing.

Douglass, Frederick. *Life and Times of Frederick Douglass* New York: Carol Publishing Group, 1991.

The New Crisis Magazine, January/February, 1999.

www.ingramcontent.com/pod-product-compliance
Lightning Source LLC
LaVergne TN
LVHW091552060526
838200LV00036B/797